BRINGING *Yourself* TO WORK

BRINGING *Yourself* TO WORK

A GUIDE to SUCCESSFUL
STAFF DEVELOPMENT in
AFTER-SCHOOL PROGRAMS

Michelle Seligson
and Patricia Stahl

 Teachers College,
Columbia University
New York and London

nsaca
National School-Age Care Alliance
Boston, MA and Washington, DC

18.95

Published simultaneously by Teachers College Press, 1234 Amsterdam Avenue, New York, NY 10027 and by the National School-Age Care Alliance, 1137 Washington Street, Boston, MA 02124

Library of Congress Cataloging-in-Publication Data

Seligson, Michelle, 1941–
    Bringing yourself to work : a guide to successful staff development in after-school programs / Michelle Seligson and Patricia Stahl.
       p. cm.
    Includes bibliographical references and index.
    ISBN 0-8077-4426-3 (paper)
     1. School-age child care. 2. Child care workers. 3. Group relations training. 4. Emotional intelligence. I. Stahl, Patricia (Patricia Jahoda). II. Title.
    HQ778.6.S45 2004
    362.71'2—dc22   2003060769

ISBN 0-8077-4426-3 (paper)

Printed on acid-free paper
Manufactured in the United States of America

10   09   08   07   06   05   04   03   8   7   6   5   4   3   2   1

Contents

Preface

When we met for lunch one day in the spring of 1998, brought together by our colleague Katie Wheeler for a chat about after-school programs, we had no idea we would become co-explorers in Bringing Yourself to Work: Caregiving in After-School Environments.

From the very beginning, it was clear we shared common ground. We both believed that after-school programs are one of the few remaining environments where children can be themselves, where they can discover interests and skills uniquely theirs, and where they can feel cared for and cared about. We also shared a conviction that kids benefit most from the care of self-aware, emotionally available adults, people who possess outstanding relationship skills.

We shared a passion to see after-school programs across the country become a haven for children and staff, where self-awareness, connection, and cooperation were established priorities. It did not take us long to realize that a movement was sweeping the business and education communities, a movement that promoted many of the same beliefs we wanted to introduce into the after-school community. It was called "emotional intelligence,"[1] and it caught on like wildfire.

Factories, hospitals, and Fortune 500 companies all began assessing the emotional intelligence of their employees, in many cases as a way to improve their bottom line. This was the theory: If people are more emotionally intelligent, if they understand their own feelings and emotions as well as those of others, they'll likely become more effective managers, salespeople, nurses, teachers, factory workers, and so on. As we read about the incredible impact of emotional intelligence in the workplace, we wondered if this movement could apply to a different environment: the after-school world.

After-school programs had become a very hot topic at the time, and were attracting a great deal of attention from many different sectors. In 1990, an estimated 50,000 programs were providing care for children in elementary and middle schools.[2] By 1997, the U.S. Department of Education created the first major education funding program for after-school care, called The 21st Century

Community Learning Centers Program. Educators, policy-makers, and members of law enforcement and countless other private and public-sector organizations all began looking to after-school time as a valuable way to reach children. These new players joined a group of after-school supporters and providers that had been growing for several decades in the United States, often without public funding or support.

With an unprecedented amount of interest and more government funding than ever before, by 1998 the after-school world was at a fascinating crossroads. There was money, there were supporters, and there was much dialogue among funders and program planners about the purpose of the programs.

For some, the goal of after-school programs is to raise student test scores across the country. Many people believe programs should focus their time on reading, writing, and arithmetic as a way to help children improve academically. For others, after-school programs represent an ideal way to keep children off the streets. By receiving supervision between the hours of 3 p.m. and 6 p.m., children would have fewer opportunities to experiment with sex, drugs, or alcohol, and would have access to recreational activities, homework help, and support with social and emotional problems. Still others see after-school time as valuable "down-time" where children can play, socialize, and learn life skills.[3]

As the national debate continued about the appropriate use of after-school time, we kept coming back to our vision. Whatever a program's mandate, we saw children in a safe, emotionally healthy environment where they could establish true friendships and mentoring relationships with the after-school caregivers. The self-aware staff would work as a cohesive team, and model kindness, empathy, and respect for each other and the children in the program. Staff would share their own stories. They would understand the value of connection. They could value their position as role models.

Intuitively, we knew this type of environment would benefit the staff and children, whatever the goal of the program. If the focus was on academics, having a socially and emotionally healthy environment would make academic learning possible. If the focus was on crime prevention, making sure that children bonded with caring, supportive staff would keep them coming back. At least, this is what our intuition told us. What we needed was a mountain of research that showed the very same things and that's exactly what we found.

A handful of studies compared child outcomes in a sample of after-school programs and found something encouraging: Programs that achieved good academic and social results were those in which staff related to the children with warmth and empathy.[4] In otherwise very similar programs, these studies showed how a positive relationship between the caregivers and children can increase the chances of learning and personal growth. And this was just the tip of the iceberg.

Evaluations of mentoring programs proved that relationships between a young person and a mentor played a significant role in improving grades, school attendance, and family relationships, as well as preventing drug and alcohol initiation. In 1997, the *Journal of the American Medical Association* reported that teenagers with at least one strong adult relationship had the best chance of being healthy and avoiding high-risk behaviors, such as crime, drug use, and pregnancy.[5]

We delved deeper into the research and found that writing on emotional intelligence in the workplace and schools was being widely published. Relational theory, developed at the Wellesley College Stone Center, was also giving us insight into the value of human connection, an important component of working with children.

We also found evidence in education research[6] that supported a core belief of what eventually became *Bringing Yourself to Work*—that the best teachers relate to their students *from the perspective of their own experience.* These teachers carry memories of being a child with them every day. They can vividly recall their experiences at recess, with playground bullies, homework, and many of the other day-to-day realities of childhood and adolescence. They then use these recollections and personal experiences to relate to children in a sensitive and empathetic way.

In all of the literature we read, across all of the different disciplines, perhaps the most exciting discovery was that *emotional intelligence can be learned.*[7] In other words, warm and talented caregivers, like the ones described above, aren't just born that way. People can learn to build quality relationships with children and fellow staff members. They can be taught to make connections with others, to understand the importance of self-awareness, and to encourage self-awareness among children. In short, after-school caregivers can be taught to create an environment where all children—troubled or "difficult" children, talented children who have had few opportunities to shine, children waiting for an opportunity to connect with a nurturing adult—can finally find what they are waiting for.

For us, the next question was, where do we go from here? If emotional intelligence can be taught, as we found out that it could, how could we get this information into the after-school community?

We began looking at different training curricula in the field of education to see what kind of information caregivers-in-training were already receiving about emotional intelligence, self-awareness, and building connections. We knew that school-age child care programs had national quality standards that emphasized the importance of self-awareness for staff, but often only in passing. Some national training organizations also included mention in their training curricula of the need for sensitivity and respect, but they were usually just brief comments and little more.

We believed we needed an *emphasis* on emotional intelligence and all its components in the after-school world—not in passing, but front and center. Why? While the research told us that this environment would lead to better outcomes for children and staff, we had more personal experiences that led us to that conclusion as well.

For Pat, there were a number of emotional experiences that stood out, both in her personal life, as the mother of two young boys, and in her professional work with children. She told the story of Peter, a shy, awkward 15-year-old who joined the Boston Children's Museum Adolescent Work Program with a painfully low level of self-confidence. His intended role at the museum was to talk to visitors at a science exhibit, but staff members quickly realized how difficult that would be for Peter, who usually stood quietly by himself, avoiding eye contact whenever he could.

Pat witnessed Susan, a compassionate staff member and one-time shy child herself, taking the time to talk with Peter, and to find out what he liked about science. Susan also shared stories with him about being bashful at his age, and gave him tips to overcome his fear of public speaking. The end result was one few could have predicted: Peter's booth on centrifugal force was a smashing success and his self-confidence rose dramatically.

In this case, and in many more throughout her career, Pat saw how a caring adult could positively affect a child. Their self-esteem could grow, or they could feel more comfortable in a care setting, all because a staff member took the extra time to understand them. In hearing Pat's stories, Michelle realized how similar they were to her own experience as she traveled throughout the country researching after-school programs in the early years of the School-Age Child Care Project (now the National Institute on Out-of-School Time) based at the Wellesley Centers for Women. The programs she loved weren't those with the fanciest facilities or the most equipment. They were those places where warmth and connection between the staff members and the children created an environment where she herself felt welcomed, included, and as if she were a part of the family.

In addition to our personal and professional motivations, there was another reason we knew this project had to go forward: In the heart of Charleston, South Carolina, we found a remarkable after-school program called Wings for kids®. Housed in Memminger Elementary School, this 3-year-old after-school program works with 120 children, almost all from low-income families, and teaches them and the staff about emotional intelligence and many of the other philosophies we discuss in *Bringing Yourself to Work*. The Wings for kids® staff consists mostly of college students, some of whom have never worked with school-age children before, but all of whom are learning about emotional intelligence as part of their training.

As we wrote *Bringing Yourself to Work*, the Wings for kids® program was a constant source of inspiration, as were five after-school programs in Massachusetts we asked to help us understand the intricacies of after-school life. Quotes from the staff of these and other programs, along with our firsthand observations of the staff at work, are woven throughout this book.

There are stories of children who started out the school year very shy and distant, and who had clearly bonded with their caregivers. We watched as one of these children draped his arms around his caregiver, resting his head on the caregiver's back for an entire 20-minute assembly. We watched another child, an 8-year-old girl, deliver a Maya Angelou poem to a small group of adults in the gymnasium with a remarkable level of confidence and passion. The moment became even more poignant after the girl's mother told us how painfully introverted her daughter was before joining the program. She credits her daughter's newfound confidence to the attention and support of the Wings for kids® staff.

The more we looked at Wings for kids® and the other programs we visited, the more connections we saw. And the more we observed the caregivers and directors in each one, the more we realized that quality relationships between staff and children don't happen by accident. Rather, making connections requires commitment. It requires a conscious, intentional effort by administrators and staff to build an environment where children and staff can reach out to one another in an atmosphere of safety and trust.

After all our research, both in the field and in the library, we realized this: Creating connections between caregivers and children is *magical*, not *magic*. *Bringing Yourself to Work* is our attempt to take away the mystery, and to give you the tools to begin creating a caring social and emotional learning environment in your program or center.

Enjoy the journey.

MICHELLE SELIGSON
PATRICIA STAHL
Boston, Massachusetts
September 2003

Acknowledgments

Bringing Yourself to Work was made possible by the contributions of a number of people who shared ideas, support, resources and, above all, the vision of what the project could mean to the after-school program field. To develop an approach to staff training that ventures into the world of the psyche and spirit was not an easy task to conceptualize. We are grateful to Katie Wheeler who was there at the conception and helped guide the initial field research and literature review phase of the project with skill and energy. Lisa Sjostrom also helped us capture our ideas for this book in an early draft, and we are grateful to her.

It goes without saying that the strong support we received from our three funders made it all possible, and we experienced their faith in us to explore this topic as a major factor in our being able to bring the ideas to fruition. Thank you, Diana Barrett, trustee of the Gioconda and Joseph King Foundation; Pamela and Hunter Boll, of the foundation that bears their name; and an anonymous foundation for their generosity and support. We worked long and hard to refine our ideas, gather and analyze the research, and craft new and relevant experiential exercises. Foremost, we thank Dr. Cathy Heenan for joining us, and giving so much of herself to the development of this work. Her pioneering work with after-school staff over the years has paved the way for this book. Our plan to integrate theories from several intellectual bases depended on the wonderful ideas we learned about from the Relational Theory group at the Stone Center at Wellesley Centers for Women. Jean Baker Miller and Judy Jordan gave of their time and encouragement even before we had attempted to write a single word. Meeting up with folks from the world of emotional intelligence, and indirectly, with the work of Peter Salovey, Dan Goleman, and others was also an important confirmation that we were on the right track.

The initial review of the research was conducted by Mary Casey and Jennifer Ekert, of the Harvard Graduate School of Education. We are in their debt for getting us started on the continuous learning process that unearthed new research and ideas. Without Marybeth Macphee, the final version of the research review,

The Relevance of Self at Work: Emotional Intelligence and Staff Training in After-School Environments, would not have been as interesting or rich a document as it is. Marybeth was our friend and colleague and emotional ballast during the first year of the project. Barbara Doyle joined us in year 2, and has helped especially as we got started with our trainings and in the search for a publisher, and we thank her very much.

To Paul Welsh, Patti Schom-Moffatt, Lianne Kerr, and all the people on the Karyo team—what else is there to say but a profound thank you. Their technical and conceptual help in all aspects of the work continues to clarify our ideas, translate them into useable material, and help us envision the future of our work.

To the directors of the five programs in Massachusetts we visited and who came to meetings at Wellesley College and allowed us to try out our model as it developed, thank you Sydney and Linda, Ed, Judy, Pam, and Roberta for your personal and professional gifts to us. We hope you find this book both representative of your own views and also a help to your staff. Ginny Deerin, and the staff at Wings for kids® permitted us to visit and video, and we hope, to capture some of the essence of a program totally dedicated to using the principles of emotional intelligence on a daily basis. You have been an inspiration to us, and we thank you. We express our appreciation to Jenny Amory, former director of Massachusetts School-Age Coalition (MSAC), for organizing a focus group so we could touch base with after-school providers in the Boston area. Mickey thanks Victor Kazanjian and Dick Nodell for our partnership on the Leading from Within workshop at Wellesley, an idea that seeded what became *Bringing Yourself to Work*.

To the many people in the after-school field who wrote to us after finding our web site, told us they had been waiting for such a project, and asked when it would be ready so they could use this kind of training on relationships with their staff, thank you for having the enthusiasm and the generosity of spirit to let us know we were on the right track.

To Barry, Max, Gabriel, Sally, and Jon. Thank you for being our family and for teaching us about relationships, connection, and love.

BRINGING *Yourself* TO WORK

Chapter One

Bringing Yourself to Work

Model for Change

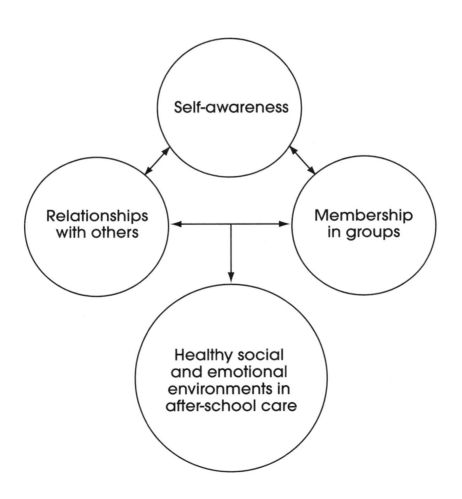

> By perceiving ourselves as part of the river, we accept responsibility for the river as a whole.
>
> —Vaclav Havel (1983, *Letters to Olga*, p. 301)

A MODEL FOR CHANGE IN AFTER-SCHOOL CARE

We can all remember workplaces where everything is clicking. Coworkers enjoy one another's company, people can count on one another, and people feel safe sharing ideas and taking risks. Leaders have a sense of when to lead and when to follow. Authority and power are shared and people know their role and their place. It's energizing, it feels right, and in an after-school program, it shows in the relationships between the caregivers and the children. But chances are, it hasn't happened by accident. Someone or something was in place to create a culture where everyone (staff, administrators, children, parents) could thrive and grow.

On the other hand, we've all been in workplaces where something's missing. These are places where work always feels like drudgery and it's not safe to challenge authority, where you save your ideas for another time. Your job saps your energy, and you can't wait until it's time to go home.

So what's the difference? We believe, as do others, that it rests in giving people the support and mechanisms they need to be authentic at work, to forge deeper connections with others, and to understand their role as members of a group. And that's where *Bringing Yourself to Work* comes into play. *Bringing Yourself to Work* is a new training model for after-school caregivers with a basic premise: Having better relationships with others starts by having a better understanding of yourself. That means knowing your strengths and weaknesses, "what pushes your buttons," what makes you defensive or joyous, anxious or depressed.

Why is this important? Because we don't exist in this world alone. Our day is made up of countless interactions at home, at work, and at play. We send hundreds of signals to people each day, and as a caregiver in after-school programs, the messages you send are particularly important. Children are watching you, and more important, they're learning from you. Your behavior matters. *Understanding* that caregivers are role models matters. Knowing that the children are your witnesses makes you want to be the best possible leader, care provider, mentor, coach, and friend.

Our training model (shown on the previous page) will assist after-school caregivers to develop a greater sense of who they are and how they relate to one another, both as individuals and as members of a group. The outcome: the creation of healthier social and emotional learning environments for children in after-school care where they feel a sense of connection to and support from the adults who care for them.

Our model for change builds on three fundamental ideas:

1. Increased self-awareness is the first step in developing mutually empowering relationships with others. We need to explore who we are and what affects our emotions if we are to develop stronger relationships with others, whether it be with coworkers or the children in our care.

2. Increased self-awareness can be learned. We all have the capacity to become more self-aware and simply need the tools and the guidance to build on the raw material that is in all of us.

3. Building our capacity for increased self-awareness is a continual process of improvement. It takes work, time, and ongoing training and support.

We also believe that staff in any program looking to adopt our model for change needs to understand some guiding principles that must be present if the model is to be successful. You need to believe that:

- We are all capable of change.
- We can recognize, acknowledge, and work with the obstacles to our changing.
- We can engage in productive self-reflection in the workplace.
- We can affect each other.
- We can treat each other with empathy and respect for differences.
- We have a defined mission in caregiving that serves as continued guidance as we set and work toward our goals.

Our model for change is not about self-exposure. We are not suggesting that your staff meetings become therapy sessions where people reveal their deepest and darkest secrets. We are, however, talking about acknowledging the important part that our emotions, our history and self-knowledge, and our capacity for empathy play in our ability to work effectively with others. We are also talking about increasing self-awareness in relation to your role as a caregiver and all that role implies as a coworker, role model, team member, colleague, friend, coach, mentor, administrator, and leader. We are talking about acknowledging the real, human, and personal interaction that takes place in after-school programs, and harnessing the power of these interactions in order to grow and learn.

BUILDING FROM A FOUNDATION

Our model for change builds on some of the most important thinking in the areas of developmental psychology, emotional intelligence, social and emotional learning, relational theory, social relations, group relations, and organizational development.

Bringing Yourself to Work is unique in that we locate this theoretical thinking within the after-school care community. Our model for change takes theory and puts it into practice; ours is a model of continual self-improvement, not only in terms of increased self-awareness, but in terms of improved relations with others and a better understanding of how the self must find a place in the dynamics of a larger group. We also believe our model for change will lead to tangible outcomes in terms of healthier social and emotional learning environments for children, child care staff, parents, support staff, and administrators.

So how did we arrive at this model for change? Which areas of research influenced our thinking?

Developmental Psychology

To begin with, the research in the area of quality child and youth care is almost unanimous in its support of the notion that quality boils down to the quality of the relationships between the adults and the children in their care.

In their book *From Neurons to Neighborhoods: The Science of Early Child Development*, Jack P. Shonkoff and Deborah A. Phillips look at the various forces and influences that shape young people's lives. They write that "young children whose caregivers provide ample verbal and cognitive stimulation, who are sensitive and responsive, who give them generous amounts of attention and support are more advanced in all realms of development compared with children who fail to receive these important inputs." They also found that the stability and skill of the care providers appear to go together and state that "more stable providers have been found to engage in more appropriate, attentive, and engaged interactions with the children in their care." When looking at the field of youth work, Shonkoff and Phillips found that "successful prevention programs are most often locally developed and implemented by adults who have long-lasting and committed relationships with the youth within the communities these programs serve." They go on to say that successful youth programs "operate in settings that encourage practitioners to build strong relationships based on mutual trust and respect."[1]

With similar findings, Renee Spencer, of the Stone Center for Research at Wellesley College, makes a strong case for the primary importance of the adult-child relationship to the overall well-being of a child. When looking at the research around child care and youth programs, Spencer points out that "the conclusion that it was the adult leadership that distinguished the programs that were successful suggests that who delivers the service and how may be more important than the particular format or structure of the intervention itself."[2] In other words, it's not just about the physical surroundings. It's not about the amount of time devoted to a particular activity. It's about the connection between the staff person and the children.

Given the importance of the relationship between a care provider and a child, we asked ourselves a question: What makes one care provider connect with the children while another doesn't? We believe it comes down to increasing the capacity for self-awareness, building stronger connections with others, and understanding one's role within a group. And many of the leading thinkers we came across in our research agree.

Emotional Intelligence

It is impossible to talk about self-awareness and stronger connections in the workplace without talking about emotional intelligence. The term *emotional intelligence* was first made popular by former *New York Times* reporter Daniel Goleman in his best-selling book *Emotional Intelligence*.[3] Emotional intelligence is loosely defined as a set of traits that helps people recognize and understand their own thoughts, feelings, and behavior, as well as those of other people. Just as people can have a high IQ—an "intelligence quotient" that represents their academic capabilities—they can also have a high EQ—an "emotional quotient," which represents a different kind of intelligence. One deals with *book* smarts, the other deals more with *social* smarts.

Goleman's thesis is that more often than not, our EQ is more important than our IQ. If making our way in the world is just about our ability to comprehend and process information, why do we have examples of incredibly gifted people who cannot cope or thrive, and why do we have examples of the C student or the college dropout who rises to the top of his or her chosen field?

Goleman says the ability to know ourselves, understand our emotions and how those emotions affect the people around us, is important if we are to meet the changing demands of work and relationships. Goleman also makes the point that emotional intelligence can be learned and, in turn, taught. Unlike our IQ, which can be increased only to our teenage years, Goleman and others argue that at any age we have the capacity to increase our emotional intelligence. It takes training, support, and the ability to stand back and take a neutral, objective look at our emotions in a given situation and how those emotions affect our experience and the experience of those around us. Goleman's work builds on the work and thinking of many people working in the field of emotional intelligence, such as Peter Salovey and John Mayer, Hendrie Weisinger, and Martin Seligman.[4]

Social and Emotional Learning

Building on the premise that emotional intelligence can be learned, Goleman and other leading thinkers in the education field believe our schools are the place where emotional intelligence should first be taught. Goleman was one of the founders of the Collaborative to Advance Social and Emotional Learning (CASEL), an organization of researchers devoted to moving social and emotional learning from the fringes to the center of our education system and curricula.

Social and emotional learning is really emotional intelligence applied. Supporters of social and emotional learning argue that how children feel and what is happening in a child's life directly affects his or her ability to be attentive while at school. Recognizing the social and emotional needs of students requires increased self-awareness and understanding among teachers and they must be given the training and support they need to increase these skills.

In his book, *Educating Minds and Hearts: Social and Emotional Learning and the Passage into Adolescence*, Jonathan Cohen surveys the area of social and emotional learning in education and makes this observation:

> In recent years, teachers and researchers have rediscovered what good teachers and parents have known for many years; that knowledge of ourselves and others, as well as the capacity to use this knowledge to solve problems creatively, provides an essential foundation for both academic learning and the capacity to become an active, constructive citizen.

Cohen and others in the social and emotional learning movement believe it is crucial for schools to create a process that allows time for self-reflection and learning among staff: "It is useful to recognize that what we do as teachers is based on our past experiences as well as on the conscious and unrecognized facets of our currents lives," Cohen says.[5] He also goes on to make the point that as with any other group, the relationship between teachers and students is mutual. What the students do and say in the classroom or on the playground affects teachers and, in turn, the teachers' reactions affect the students.

Exploring the nature of these actions and reactions and what they mean to both teachers and students alike is one of the central points of social and emotional learning. We believe it is the nature of these same types of interactions between caregivers and children that lead to the creation of healthy social and emotional learning environments in after-school programs.

Relational Theory

Like many of these thinkers, we see self-awareness as the building block of emotional intelligence. But our model for change has also been influenced by scholars of relational theory who place importance on understanding who we are in relation to others. Rather than viewing people as a group of individual free-agents, relational theory argues that we grow and learn through our interactions with others. Jean Baker Miller, Judith Jordan, Renee Fletcher, Joyce Fletcher, and others at the Stone Center for Research at Wellesley College argue that it is our ability to create meaningful connections with others, to be authentic, and to create a sense of mutual empathy that allows us to grow as individuals.[6]

Judith Jordan describes the idea of mutual empathy as mutuality. What does mutuality mean? It's the ability to join another person in his or her feelings and have the person join you in yours. It's not simply active listening, nor is it a one-way street where we feel empathy for another person. Mutuality means that we feel respect and empathy for the other person and, at the same time, experience this same feeling coming from the other person to us. Creating mutual empathy leads to mutual empowerment, where both people feel a greater sense of connection and understanding.

Jean Baker Miller defines five outcomes of good connection—outcomes that she describes as a source of energy with other people and a source of power to transform a person's experience with another, whether it is with a partner, co-worker, or friend. The five outcomes are zest, increased self-esteem, a desire for more connection, increased knowledge of self and others, and an increased desire and ability to act. Because we are energized by the exchange, we want more—to be more truthful, more open and honest—all because we feel from the other person that he or she wants and expects the same from us.

For our model of *Bringing Yourself to Work* to be successful, after-school workers must develop a greater understanding of who they are in relation to the people with whom they work. The personal demands of child care work are enormous—and so are the personal rewards—and creating more meaningful connections between coworkers, and between leaders and staff, will translate into the ability to develop more meaningful relationships with the children in their care.

Group Relations/Organizational Development

Finally, in developing our model for change, we examined how knowing more about ourselves and how we relate to others plays itself out within the dynamics of the larger group in an after-school center or program. As we all know, after-school care is group work: the program or center is a group; the children are in groups; center staff are in groups. Add parents, janitors, funders, and people from the community, and you see just how many different interests and points of view need to be juggled each and every day.

Building on theory in the fields of group relations and organizational development, our model for change says that program providers and administrators need to know that groups have an unconscious life of their own. Therefore, we need the tools to understand that things happen in a group we can't predict, and we need to be aware of what we can control and what we can't.

Leading organizational behavior thinkers, such as Larry Hirschhorn, and organizations, such as the A. K. Rice Institute, argue convincingly about the need for organizations to do a better job of understanding how groups work and how individuals thrive within those groups.[7] While their focus is on how businesses can be successful in a changing economy, we believe their ideas have important implications for the after-school environment. Following their lead, we need to rethink our notions about authority, how we forge connections in the workplace, how we communicate, build a sense of vision and team, and acknowledge dependence on one another.

This brief overview of theory from the fields of organizational development, group relations, relational theory, emotional intelligence, and developmental psychology presents a glimpse into just some of the information that opened up to us as we began to explore our own ideas about the after-school environment. What we found was that we were not alone. People in every field and every industry are talking about the very same ideas about healthy human development and organizational life as we are. There is a change happening out there. And we hope *Bringing Yourself to Work* will be a new lens through which to view your life and your role as a participant in the after-school care community.

HOW THIS BOOK IS ORGANIZED

The remaining chapters of this book explore each of the elements of our model for change in more detail and encourage you to imagine how the ideas behind *Bringing Yourself to Work* can be applied in your own lives and in your own after-school program. In Chapter 2 the focus is on developing your self-awareness. Then we turn to helping you to build relationships with others (Chapter 3) and to see yourself as a member of a group (Chapter 4). Chapter 5 deals with the concept of change. The appendix consists of a self-assessment tool that you can use to measure where you and your program are now and to evaluate your progress as you work through our model for change.

Through a series of case studies in Chapters 2-4, we introduce you to some of the children and staff from Wings for kids®, that exciting after-school program, we mentioned previously. Wings for kids® is a real, living example of the *Bringing Yourself to Work* model in action, and is an inspiration to all of us about what is possible when strong mutually beneficial relationships are forged between caregivers and children.

In some of the other examples of after-school programs in this book, names and locations of centers and staff have been changed to protect their identities. In other cases, examples are composites of different programs, centers, and staff we have encountered as part of our research and are meant to illustrate our ideas and bring them to life. In Chapters 2–4, we give you some useful exercises—what we call "Next Steps"—to help you start applying these ideas in your own life right away.

At the end of Chapters 2–4 we list selected readings for those of you who want to find out more about the concepts and ideas that provide the foundations for *Bringing Yourself to Work*. We've only been able to provide an introduction to these thinkers, but their work provides valuable insights and experiences for anyone committed to caring for our children in a different way.

Chapter Two

Becoming More Self-Aware

Model for Change

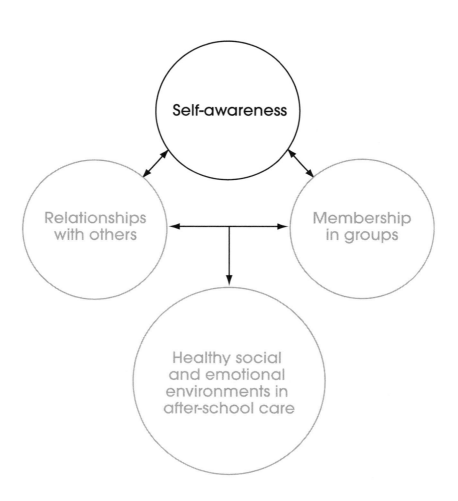

I observe myself and so I come to know others

—Lao Tse

THE IMPORTANCE OF EMOTIONAL INTELLIGENCE

Sarah is an after-school caregiver in Boston, and she loves her job. She's worked with children for 11 years, first as a special-education teacher and now as an after-school caregiver who helps children with homework and special projects. There's something special about Sarah. Children gravitate toward her—they even seem to compete for her attention as she walks around the room. They excitedly show her their work, eager for the encouragement she offers. And she talks with them—really *talks* with them—about their day, about their friends, about the challenges they face at home and at school. When a child speaks, she listens as though he or she is the only one in the room. During their conversations, she shares stories about her own childhood and her own feelings, in part to help the child understand he or she is not alone and in part to remember what it was like to be that age. Sarah knows she has a lot to give—and the connections she makes with the children in her class give her as much as the children get from her.

Maria is also a caregiver, but her day-to-day experiences aren't as positive as Sarah's. Their programs share similar characteristics—they serve the same population of children and families located in nearby neighborhoods. Their program spaces could use a good coat of paint and some new furniture, but are well-equipped with arts materials, books, games, and educational activities. Both programs have a high rate of staff turnover, and both women work in the classroom with the children and are also responsible for some administrative tasks. Both advocate for better salaries and benefits with their peers in the after-school community. But even with all the similarities between them, Sarah's and Maria's experiences of work are noticeably different.

For a number of reasons, Maria doesn't connect as well as Sarah with the children in her care. Her patience runs out a little sooner in the day than she would like; she's often distracted by the unfinished administrative tasks she has on her plate; and she frequently focuses on the negative side of a situation rather than the positive. Recently, for example, a new caregiver was hired to replace yet another person who had left the program after less than 1 year. Rather than working well with the eager and hardworking new staff member, Maria could hardly find the motivation to introduce herself. She was convinced he wouldn't be there for long, and she didn't think there was anything she could do about it. As you might expect, a bond between the new caregiver and Maria didn't really form.

Maria's relationships with the children in her program reflect a similar emotional distance. Sometimes she feels too busy to talk to a child about his or her weekend because she still has a lesson plan to complete; other times she feels anxious that even more staff will leave the program. Maria also doesn't feel her own childhood experiences are relevant to share with the children or important to them, making it more difficult for them to know her, be comfortable with her, or to turn to her for emotional support or guidance. It's clear that Maria brings certain things to work—her interest in being organized and punctual, her concern that the program will have enough staff—but it's also clear that something might be missing. She feels dissatisfied. She's not connected to the children or other staff members. She feels that something's not quite right and thinks about quitting.

Given that Sarah and Maria are working in similar after-school situations, why are their experiences so very different? Why is one woman more "successful" at her job, more fulfilled, and more of a role model for the children and staff in her program than the other? These two people probably have vastly different levels of *emotional intelligence*, a concept we introduced in Chapter 1.

Case Study:
Self-Awareness at Wings for kids®

Hands down, Keisha Jones was the last kid on the block asked to baby-sit. As the youngest of four children, including two brothers, Keisha says her impatience with children was a running joke among her neighbors and family members. "The word 'motherly' certainly wasn't in my vocabulary," she says, laughing. "If you believe all the world is a stage—and that everyone has a role—my role was to be the tough guy, not the caregiver."

Although projecting a rough-and-tumble exterior may have come naturally to Keisha, it wasn't making her happy. "I realized after I entered college that whatever I was doing, however I was behaving, it wasn't working," she says. "I didn't like a lot

of things in my life, and I was looking for a way to change."

One of the steps to changing her life came during her 2nd year of college. Keisha began looking for a volunteering opportunity that would give her a sense of fulfillment, one where she could be a role model and teach kids the feelings of self-respect she learned from her parents. That's when she found Wings for kids®. She says about the program: "The Wings for kids® application form was very interesting because it asked a lot about your life experiences, your upbringing, and your philosophy on different things. In terms of raising my self-awareness, it all started there. I really started thinking about my

Unlike our IQ, which some theorists believe changes very little after our teen years, our emotional intelligence continues to grow as we learn from new and different experiences during our lifetime. In other words, emotional intelligence isn't something you're born with. It's not an all-or-nothing situation—either you're emotionally intelligent or you're not. On the contrary, with the right tools and the right guidance, emotional intelligence can be learned and developed over time. And that's good news, particularly in light of all the research that shows how important your emotional intelligence is.

Daniel Goleman, whom we introduced in Chapter 1, claims that as much as 80 percent of a person's success rests on his or her emotional intelligence. Book smarts will get you only so far, he says. A valedictorian's grades are only one indicator of a person's chances at personal and professional fulfillment. Sure, they're important—and often they are a very good indicator of how well a person will do in life—but they're not the only thing to consider. Other qualities factor in as well, such as how well a person communicates with the people in his or her life. Does he really listen? Can she sense if there's a problem even when no one has told her? Is he positive, engaged, and truthful? Is she likeable? These things aren't normally reflected on a high school transcript, but they matter just the same.

Why? Because being a valedictorian or a straight-A student shows only that a person knows how to achieve success within a certain system—an academic sys-

personality and my life in a way that I never had before."

Keisha's personal transformation continued during the 40-hour Wings for kids® training session, where she participated in a series of discussions and exercises designed to explore each person's level of self-awareness. "I remember thinking that the training sessions couldn't teach me anything about myself that I didn't already know," she says. "And I was so wrong. My wall was broken down very, very quickly."

Her first realization? "I can get really worked up over little things, just like my Dad," says Keisha. "I used to make excuses for my behavior because I thought, if he did it, it must be okay. And now I know it's not." The training also helped Keisha realize that losing the tough exterior—even just for a while—can bring about some positive results. "I've let people see my softer side,

and I like the response I'm getting. Kids hug me all the time now. They want to sit by me and hold my hand, and I know that's because I've allowed myself to be affectionate and to get really close to them."

The shift in attitude has yielded some impressive results outside of the care environment as well. "I've had the same roommate for 3 years," Keisha explains. "And sometimes I would hear that she was having problems—but always from other people, never from her directly. I think a lot of people, including my roommate, wouldn't talk to me about sensitive issues before because they didn't think I was compassionate. But that's changed now. She and I talk about stuff that we never have before."

Increasing her self-awareness also meant recognizing that her natural assertiveness can be an asset at times. For

tem such as a high school or college. Book smarts don't necessarily prepare people for the varied and complex challenges of day-to-day life, such as how to talk with your spouse, how to deliver a winning interview, or how to be a good friend, listener, or caregiver. In other words, IQ and academic credentials are only part of the recipe for success.

In the example of Sarah and Maria above, the two women might have performed equally well in high school; they may, in fact, have exactly the same IQ. But a higher EQ might explain why Sarah is more successful at her job than Maria. Sarah communicates well with both the staff and children in her program, knowing when to offer constructive advice and when to stay quiet and listen. She uses her intuition to pick up the subtle cues that a child may be tired, worried, distracted, or self-conscious. Sarah is also a positive person, one who deals with many of the same staffing and organizational challenges as Maria, but one who believes she can positively affect her own life as well as the lives of others.

As a result of these emotional intelligence skills, Sarah derives more satisfaction from her job. Not only is she able to give more of herself to the children and staff at her center, Sarah feels she gets more back from them in return.

The examples of Sarah and Maria aren't unique—we've all seen people with varying degrees of emotional intelligence skills in relating to children. Some caregivers have a seemingly magical connection to kids. They're comfortable with

---

example, kids know to bring their notebooks and pencils to Keisha's Choice Time so that they can participate in the lessons. They know that being critical of another student's artwork or hurting someone's feelings isn't okay when Keisha is around. They also know that there's a time for playfulness and a time to listen—and Keisha lets them know which is which.

"I know how to read situations better than I did before," says Keisha. "And I also know which part of my personality to bring to each. Sometimes I'm motherly, sometimes I'm strict, but I always try to put myself in the child's place, whatever the circumstances."

After meeting few other college students as confident and self-possessed as Keisha Jones, we wanted to examine the factors that contributed to her impressive increase in emotional intelligence. When did she become interested in increasing her self-awareness? How did she become so empowered? Why did she want to share her unique personality with children?

Keisha's answer to our last question was simple: After carefully reviewing her life experiences, she realized how fortunate she was. She was a young, powerful, self-respecting African-American woman with a loving family and college education. Looking around the Wings for kids® playground, and seeing so many kids who weren't as lucky, she felt compelled to make a difference.

When Keisha was filling out the application to work at Wings for kids®, she began the process of examining her emotions. One of the five characteristics of emotional intelligence, *knowing one's emotions*, helps Keisha relate to the kids in a way she hadn't before. Whether she's

them; they tell entertaining and interesting stories; they listen attentively when the children share information about their lives; there's a mutual respect and admiration between them that transcends differences in age or gender. In relationships like these, the warmth and affection is unmistakable. Far from being a magical formula—where some people "have it" and some people never will—many of these skills can be learned by developing one's emotional intelligence. It will be easier for some people than for others. For example, a person with strong feeling capacity will readily relate to the idea of emotional intelligence. However, a person with less access to his or her emotions might take longer to incorporate a new way of relating to himself or herself and to others. Both types of people can be successful in developing their emotional intelligence.

WHAT IS EMOTIONAL INTELLIGENCE COMPRISED OF?

Drawing on work by Peter Salovey, Daniel Goleman organized emotional intelligence into the five categories, listed below.[1]

1. *Knowing one's emotions.* Self-awareness—the ability to recognize a feeling as it happens—is the cornerstone of emotional intelligence and self-understanding. In other words, if you don't know how you feel or why you feel that way, you'll never truly understand yourself.

teaching a frequently distracted student ways to focus his attention or helping a young girl through her disagreement with another child, Keisha knows to put herself in the child's position. How would she feel if she were in the same situation? What does she remember about being in the third grade? By answering those questions, she's able to tune into the feelings, habits, and experiences of the kids in her program. In other words, she's beginning to *recognize emotions in others,* another area of emotional intelligence.

Keisha began tackling the *managing one's emotions* area of emotional intelligence during the initial Wings for kids® training session. That's when she realized she needed to handle certain situations differently, such as not "freaking out" because she misplaced her keys. *Motivating oneself*—the next area of emotional intelli-

gence—is something Keisha works on every day. As a person who loses focus easily, Keisha makes a conscious effort to stay on track, usually by making a list of the things she needs to do and working through it one task at a time.

The end result is that Keisha is well on her way to *handling her relationships,* the fifth area of emotional intelligence. Not only has she strengthened her connections with the children in her program, she has improved her relationships with her family and friends. By learning how to respond warmly to other people's concerns or fears, Keisha has tapped into a softer side of herself that she hardly knew existed.

2. *Managing one's emotions.* Once your self-awareness increases—and you have a better understanding of how you're feeling and acting at any given moment—the next step is to manage your behavior in more constructive, more positive ways. People who are successful in life are typically better able to manage emotions such as stress, sadness, or disappointment.

3. *Motivating oneself.* You've heard it a thousand times—there is power in positive thinking. Having a high degree of emotional intelligence is also a reflection of a person's self-control, whether that means delaying immediate gratification or staying positive in the face of challenging circumstances.

4. *Recognizing emotions in others.* Understanding how *you* feel about a situation or event might help you understand how other people would feel in a similar situation. Otherwise known as empathy, the ability to recognize the subtle cues that reveal what other people are thinking and feeling is a valuable social skill. Empathetic people tend to be more tuned in to other people, which means they can often lend the right support or say the right thing without ever being asked.

5. *Handling relationships.* Success in life also depends on how well a person interacts with others, including coworkers, friends, or family members. Goleman labels as "social stars" people who are able to organize and inspire others, reduce conflict in groups, build friendships easily, and respond warmly to other people's concerns or fears. These are the people who get along with virtually everyone else.

Imagine that there's a scale of emotional intelligence, where people understand themselves and others in degrees. Some would rank higher on the scale than others, and vice versa. While it's true that we all have the capacity to understand ourselves and each other, some people are more successful at developing and maintaining healthy, fulfilling relationships than others. Of the five areas of emotional intelligence, these people might be skilled in all five. They might be motivated, supportive, friendly, positive, and highly self-aware. Other people, however, might be strong in certain areas of emotional intelligence and not in others.

Each of us falls somewhere on the scale of emotional intelligence—high, low, or in-between. And this, in turn, affects the kind of relationships we form with others.

As caregivers, building relationships is a critical and rewarding part of the job. The research shows it, and we intuitively know it's true: The most important thing caregivers can do for children is to connect with them, to build meaningful, honest relationships where both the caregivers and children feel safe enough to share their experiences and be themselves. A key to improving these relationships, we believe, is to improve people's capacity to be emotionally intelligent, to teach them the skills they need to become aware, inspirational, caring participants in the world in which they live and work.

And that starts with having a greater sense of self-awareness.

SELF-AWARENESS: IT ALL STARTS WITH YOU

Who are you? And who is that "self" you bring to work?

It seems like a straightforward question. You might have answered that you are a woman or a man, or that you are young or old. Or you might refer to your professional identity—child care worker, recreation staff person, youth program coordinator. Or perhaps you described some attribute of yourself, such as friend, partner, reader, gardener, aunt, niece, American, African American, Californian, homeowner, commuter. Maybe you described a characteristic, such as loyal, loving, impatient, driven, sloppy, happy, sad, timid, strong, weak, reckless, caring, or aggressive.

You might have chosen an entirely different way to answer the question. You might not have even answered the question at all, and instead read on to the next paragraph. It doesn't matter what your answer was. The real point is that very few people ask themselves that question to begin with. Sure, people may take stock of themselves from time to time, but rarely do they sit down, dig deep, and ask themselves—really ask themselves—*who am I?* What makes me tick? What kind of mother, child-care worker, friend, or partner am I? What traits make up my personality? If I'm impatient, where does that come from and how does it affect the way I deal with the children I care for? If I'm creative and artistic, how can I incorporate these talents into my after-school program? If I'm not comfortable with diversity, how can I recognize those feelings and alter my behavior in more positive ways?

So, who are you?

This is the central question that we believe needs to be explored to work together more effectively, particularly in the after-school care environment where the product of our labor is the nation's young people. As an after-school care provider, whether you're working directly with children or running a program, it's time to ask yourself the question, "Who am I?" The answers may reveal how your emotions, past experiences, and relationships have shaped your life, your moods, and your relationships with others. Answering that question may also help you understand what unique characteristics and experiences you bring to the workplace and how they influence the bonds you form with coworkers and the children in your care.

In short, exploring that question is the first step toward increasing your self-awareness.

WHAT IS SELF-AWARENESS?

Self-awareness is defined as the ability to recognize, observe, and investigate our emotions from moment to moment. Simply put, being self-aware means knowing *how* you feel and *why* you feel that way. Upon first glance, this sounds reasonably straightforward. You're frustrated because your car won't work. You're anxious because your parents are coming into town. You're relieved because your coworker didn't call in sick today. But it's not always this easy. How often have you heard

> Alan
>
> "I'm a huge video game fan, and I remember times when I'd be frustrated with a game and I'd start yelling at the computer screen or banging stuff around. Now I work with kids who do exactly the same thing, who get frustrated with a game on the basketball court or on the computer. And I totally relate. I try to calm them down and explain that it's only a game. I also try to remember that myself when I'm feeling the same way."

people say that, after taking time to think about a conversation or an event, they see it differently? Or that things look better in the morning?

The reality is that, most of the time, the vast majority of us are not self-aware, or certainly not as aware as we could be. We don't often think about how we feel or why we're reacting one way or another. Instead, we have a tendency to run on "emotional auto-pilot," unconsciously reacting to situations the way we have for years. Much of our emotional life is unconscious—and that means feelings that stir within us don't always see the light of day. What looks like anger might actually be disappointment in disguise. What looks like jealousy might actually stem from deep-seated feelings of insecurity. Once triggered, the emotions that simmer beneath the threshold of awareness can have a powerful impact on how we react in certain situations.

Think back to a staff meeting you might have had when one of your coworkers got angry and raised her voice when trying to make a point. How did it make you feel? Maybe it didn't faze you in the least. Perhaps you took it personally, wondering if she was angry with you. Did you ignore the tone of the outburst altogether and focus only on the point she was trying to make? Did you have a physical reaction, maybe a racing heartbeat or a knot in the pit of your stomach that told you the conflict was going to escalate? Did you want to run out of the room to avoid the confrontation, or did you want to stay and talk it out? Did you try to resolve it peacefully and calmly, or did you become more argumentative, perhaps making accusations or taking sides?

Different emotions lurk beneath the surface of each and every one of us, causing each of us to respond differently to the same situation. And there can be a hundred different variables to explain why. A young woman we know grew up in a very loud, vocal home, where every last point was debated in a safe and supportive environment. There was no name-calling, no belittling, just honest and frank discussion about everything from world events to feelings and emotions. Understandably, someone who spent her childhood in a home like this would be more accustomed to loud, assertive debate. She might not feel an urge to flee when faced with an angry coworker; in fact, she would likely feel quite the opposite. Her ability to listen and negotiate difficult situations are two of her strengths, things she practiced over an active dinner table throughout her childhood.

We also know people who grew up in the opposite environment. In the home of another colleague, the family retreated into silence when things threatened to get too hot. To our colleague, a raised voice is something to avoid at all costs. It's not an invitation to begin a debate—it's an indication that things will only get worse. In other words, finish dinner as fast as you can and head for the TV room.

We know another person, Daniel, who grew up in one of those perfect houses where nothing was allowed to be out of place. In this perfect house, the children were constantly reminded to pick up their things and keep their rooms clean. When his parents yelled, Daniel jumped into action—beds were made, dishes were done, laundry was folded—whatever it took to meet his parents' expectations. This was his response as an adolescent, and he acknowledges that it continues to be his response when dealing with the expectations of a coworker, friend, or family member today. Even if the expectations aren't realistic, Daniel still finds himself stuck in trying to meet them in order to please others.

How about you? Can you identify how early experiences growing up affect your behavior today? For example, if you grew up with a brother or sister, think back to how you dealt with disagreements. Were you a fighter or a peacemaker? Did you always have to have the last word? Did you always need to be right? Now think about how you deal with conflict as an adult. Do you see any similarities between your behavior back then and the way you deal with disagreements today? If you're like most people, chances are you will. At least occasionally, most of us default to our emotional comfort zones, to patterns of behavior that we developed long ago as children or adolescents. For example, the response that Daniel developed—always meeting others' expectations—is the same response he repeats as an adult.

Emotional patterns can occur with any number of behaviors—everything from how we express our anger, disappointment, confidence, or fear to why we're always on time, why we're generous, or why we find it difficult to accept compliments, criticism, or advice.

Leah, a program director we know, recently explored her emotional pattern with *avoidance*, especially when paying her parking tickets. To this day, her strategy is to ignore them. She plucks the bright yellow ticket from underneath her windshield wiper and promptly puts it, along with all the others, in her glove compartment. Invariably, she'll receive a series of warning notices over the next few months, informing her that the fine is steadily increasing. At some point, Leah will pay the fine—usually when it's more than double its original amount. In telling us this story, she realized she also has a similar strategy when renting videos. If it's a 1-day rental, she returns it in 3 days. If it's a 2-day rental, she returns it 5 days. She jokes that, for her, renting a movie costs the same as buying one.

> **Keisha**
>
> "Before, if I was having a bad day, I might lose my patience with the kids or overreact to certain situations. And I used to think I was allowed to act that way because I was in a bad mood. But that sends a message to the kids that, if they're having a tough time, they can come to Wings and take it out on me or the other students—and that's just not okay. Now I tell the kids if I'm stressed out or tired so that, hopefully, they'll do the same with me. That way I can understand where they're coming from and be sensitive if they're having a tough day."

Why does she do this? Surely it doesn't make any financial sense. We should also mention that this is, in virtually every other way, a responsible, intelligent woman who pays her rent, her car payment, and all her other bills on time. So what's going on here?

It took her some time, but Leah recognized a pattern in her life where, by and large, difficult situations in the past have just worked themselves out without much effort from her. If she felt her boyfriend was being unreasonable, for example, she would walk away from the discussion until the next day when, for whatever reason, he often came around to see her side. When she didn't have the $500 to replace the radiator in her old, orange Volvo, she left the car in the garage. One week later, her mother (an exceedingly generous woman who loved helping out the "starving student") slipped her the money.

The parking tickets are, of course, an exception. No one is magically paying the parking tickets on her behalf. The parking authorities are not writing her a letter, apologizing for the mistake and clearing away the debt. Unlike some situations in her past, Leah knows this situation will not work itself out on its own. She needs to pay the fine and she will. But it takes countless reminders for her to spring into action, to awaken to the reality that she needs to act. She needs to pay the fine or, better yet, she needs to find better (i.e., legal) parking spots.

What's interesting is that, even after recognizing this pattern, Leah still plucks the bright yellow parking tickets from underneath her windshield wiper and places them in her glove compartment. For whatever reason, she's comfortable with this process. But that doesn't mean that nothing has changed. Quite the contrary. Leah is now aware that she has a tendency to bury her head in the sand. Although she may still ignore her parking debts until the 11th hour, she is careful to deal with other, more important situations in a timely manner, even if they're unpleasant. If a parent misses two payments to her center, for example, she is quick to contact him or her to discuss the situation. If the center's landlord still hasn't fixed the large crack in the roof, she makes another call to his office. If the study guides arrive 6 weeks after their scheduled date, she calls the distributor for an explanation.

The challenge in situations like these—family disagreements, avoiding parking tickets—is to recognize the choices we have. We don't have to run on emotional autopilot. We don't have to react the same way to disappointment or avoidance or exclusion or fear as we have in the past. For example, Daniel can discuss his realization with his mother or coworkers and explain that he is trying to approach conflict differently. Then, each time he is confronted with someone speaking angrily, he can consciously choose whether to stay and discuss the situation, or state that he would rather discuss the matter once the person has calmed down. In the case of Leah, she can recognize her tendency to avoid unpleasant situations and, as she does, make sure not to avoid other, more important things in her life and in her work, like paying her student loan or having a difficult conversation with a center staff member. She may continue accruing parking tickets, but her awareness of that tendency may motivate her to stay on top of other areas of her life.

It's important to note that recognizing our emotional patterns and becoming more self-aware isn't just about identifying ways to change or improve our behavior. It's also about recognizing the special and unique qualities we already possess to ensure we also bring those to work. Take a moment to ask yourself what you're passionate about. Guitar-playing? Gardening? Hiking? Movies? How could your work experience be enhanced if caregivers shared their interests with the children through a special activity? Take a moment to think about your strengths, about the things you do well. Do you have a knack for storytelling? Are you a really good listener? Do you explain things clearly so that even challenging lessons are easy to understand? By being more aware of your personal strengths and talents, you can make sure you share them with others.

We know a caregiver in Florida named Miko who is an exceptional athlete, not only because she excels at virtually every sport she tries, but because she genuinely enjoys teaching others how to play—everything from hitting a baseball to dribbling a soccer ball to jumping hurdles. She told us that she tries to bring the same energy and patience to her students that her father brought to her when she was a child. Growing up, Miko's father would take her and her younger sister to an open field where they would practice hitting golf balls for hours. The secondhand clubs were old and heavy (they weighed almost as much as Miko's younger sister), and their shots never went very far, but her father patiently explained the sport of golf from start to finish: the grip, the swing, the rules, everything. Today, Miko does the same with her students for all sorts of different sports. The feeling of watching children "get it"—whether it's sinking their first basket or running their best 100 meters ever—reminds her of this special gift she has to share.

> **Alan**
>
> If you walk by the school cafeteria on certain Fridays, listen closely. You'll probably hear music radiating from a small, portable CD player, most likely a snappy Elvis number or the Blues Brothers version of "Shake a Tail Feather." That's because Alan brings his love of music to the school's weekly cleanup sessions. "The kids are dancing, I'm singing away, and I'm pretty sure it makes everyone work harder. And if it's a really special occasion, I'll do a little dance routine—just to get a laugh."
>
> Alan's childhood experiences explain a lot about him, such as why he knows nothing about cars and why his three-egg omelets are a work of art. As a kid, working alongside his father in the garage wasn't really an option. "I was always 'in his light' apparently," laughs Alan. "So my mother pulled me into the kitchen, strapped an apron on me, and taught me to cook." Now Alan shares his culinary wizardry with the Wings for kids® children once a week in a class that he helped create. "It feels really good to be able to share that side of myself, because maybe one of these kids will discover a love of cooking like I did."

WHAT SELF-AWARENESS IS NOT

We've done a lot of talking about what self-awareness *is*. Let's take a moment to look at what self-awareness *is not*.

Self-awareness is not about giving free reign to your feelings or letting it all hang out. Knowing that you're the type of person who angers easily doesn't give you permission to blow up when you feel like it. In fact, once you know that about yourself, you'll want to be careful about how and when you express anger. Knowing that you have a deep need to connect with other people doesn't make it permissible to share personal, intimate feelings with acquaintances, coworkers, or random strangers whenever the urge strikes you. For some topics, there is a time, a place, and an audience that need to be considered. Once you know this about yourself, you'll want to check whether or not people are interested in discussing the topic before you begin.

Self-awareness means understanding your emotions and using that knowledge to make better decisions about how to act or react. It means recognizing how and when you express yourself and knowing what form that takes. Increased self-awareness means having the ability to shift gears, to step back from a situation, to process what's going on, and *then* act. It's about weighing your choices and options, and then moving forward.

Self-awareness is not about suppressing your feelings and emotions. At its most basic level, self-awareness is about understanding what makes you who you are. It's about exploring and understanding all the different parts of yourself—both the parts you like and, perhaps, the parts you don't. Keeping a lid on your real self saps your energy and, more importantly, hides parts of yourself that, given a supportive environment, you could work to improve.

In the end, self-awareness is about balance. It's about finding safe, honest ways to be who you are and encouraging others and yourself to accept and appreciate you for all that entails.

WHY IS SELF-AWARENESS IMPORTANT?

With some time and some work each of us can learn to become more self-aware and to recognize all the different things we bring to work. But the question is: Why would you want to become more self-aware? What's in it for you?

With greater self-knowledge, you can become a better pilot of your life. Becoming more self-aware means having a stronger sense of how you feel about personal and professional details, both big and small. This means you can make better decisions regarding everything from whom to marry to which job to take or, in the case of an after-school program, how best to deal with difficult situations, such as a disruptive child.

In the case of a disruptive child, the difference between a care provider who is more self-aware and one who is less self-aware can often be seen in their responses to the child. The person who is less self-aware may respond inappropriately—giving the child ultimatums or focusing on the disruptive child at the expense of the larger group. This caregiver may lose his patience more quickly, and may not know how to refocus the child's attention on the task at hand.

The caregiver who is more self-aware—the better pilot of her emotions—may have the same feelings of irritation with a child's disruptive behavior. The difference is that the self-aware person is also able to step back, to recognize which of her emotions the child is triggering, and to take a more appropriate course of action to deal with the child. The more self-aware caregiver would focus on the deed rather than the doer. She might find a distraction for the child and channel the child's energy in a more positive way. The situation, then, becomes less about the caregiver responding to an emotional trigger of her own and more about determining what's best for the child. This can happen only if the caregiver is aware of her own feelings and how she might be able to respond in ways that are positive for both herself and the child in her care.

Achieving mastery over your emotions is freeing. Becoming more self-aware removes the mystery about how you're feeling. If you know what causes you to become impatient, worried, or rude, for example, then you're one step closer to knowing how to refine your behavior in more constructive or appropriate ways. In other words, you can alter your behavior in more positive ways once you're aware of it.

Increased self-awareness also means you can choose to act differently. Imagine you're dealing with a parent who picks up his child late at least once each week, causing you to be late for dinner with your own family. Each time the parent shows up, you assess all the different ways you could react—everything from ignoring the issue altogether to yelling, "You must promise never to be late again!" to fantasizing about receiving a big bouquet of flowers as a peace offering the next time he's late.

In the seconds during which you're assessing all your different options, everything from the reasonable to the ridiculous, you're not on emotional autopilot. You're not reacting the same way you always have—instead, you're using this time to assess your options to make a calmer, more conscious choice. Perhaps you'll choose to explain to the parent that picking up his child late causes you to be late for a class you are taking, or upsets your own family's dinner routine. You may choose to let it go this time. You might choose to send home a notice explaining the program's policy that parents whose children are at the center past a certain hour are subject to additional charges. The bottom line is that your emotions don't get the better of you and you resolve the situation differently—which, in this case, means you may not be getting any flowers, but you will be getting home on time.

WHY IS SELF-AWARENESS IMPORTANT IN AN AFTER-SCHOOL SETTING?

Every time children walk through the doors of an after-school program, they're soaking up as much information as they can. They're watching and listening, taking cues and picking up signals. They're paying attention to everything they see and hear, and in the process, they're learning lessons about a number of different things, including sharing, fairness, honesty, and participation. By interacting with caregivers and other children, they are learning how to be a friend, how to be empathetic, how to resolve conflict, and how to embrace differences. All of these lessons will shape the kinds of people they become and, in turn, will affect how they make their way in the world. In light of that, the "self" that caregivers bring to work matters.

Why? Because *we teach what we are,* according to Anabel Jensen, president of Six Seconds, a nonprofit organization devoted to the development of emotional intelligence in families, school, and communities.[2] If you are patient, you teach patience, either through an activity or by the calm, understanding way you deal with children and staff every day. If you are unfair, the children will learn how it feels to be treated unfairly and, in turn, to treat others unfairly. If you are curious, the children will become curious, following your lead as you uncover hidden mysteries in the pages of a book or under a magnifying glass. The self you bring to work is the same self the children watch and learn from. So, the question is, What are they learning from you?

At one child-care center, the program leader, Ann, understands the power of her role as a mentor and role model. For her, the children's entry into the classroom each afternoon is the most important moment of the day. This is the time for children to feel welcomed, to be acknowledged, and to feel special, even if it's just for a moment. Rather than busy herself with preparation as the kids come in, she makes herself a cup of tea and sits patiently in a small chair—right at the kids' level—welcoming each child in turn.

She listens to stories about their brothers or sisters, comments when they're wearing a new sweater, or welcomes them back if they've been away ill. It's a one-to-one moment, and the smiles on the children's faces and the hugs Ann receives prove that her ritual is working. The entire program feels right, and many parents recognize Ann's welcome as a special feature that gives this program a sense of warmth. Is Ann unique? Probably not. Many of you already know the importance of recognizing the children as they arrive. But Ann makes this a priority activity because she remembers her own memories of being a child, of entering a dance class with a room full of strangers and feeling uncomfortable. She remembers how awkward she felt and makes a conscious effort not to repeat the same experience for the children in her care.

Acknowledging children and making them feel important is Ann's primary focus. For another caregiver, the emphasis might be on encouraging tolerance and diversity. By helping children see things from another person's perspective, this caregiver helps them break down stereotypes and embrace personal and cultural differences. For yet another caregiver, it might be teaching compassion and friendship. When a child is hurt on the playground, for example, this caregiver consoles the child with a hug—a very different tactic than the "just get up and dust yourself off" line he heard throughout his childhood. He tells the child he's sorry this happened and asks if there's anything that might make her feel better. This caregiver doesn't blame or finger-point. He's just there to comfort and lend support.

Modeling these and other positive behaviors requires caregivers who are self-aware and conscious of their impact on the ways children feel about themselves, about other kids, and about the world around them. After-school programs, then, with their many mandates, aren't just places to help children with their homework or watch them while their parents are at work. They can also be places to help kids figure out who they are and how to make their way in the world. They can be places that influence human beings, their personalities, their goals, and their chances of success. They can also be one of the most rewarding places any of us could imagine working.

FOR FURTHER READING

Goleman, D. (1997). *Emotional intelligence* (pp. 13–55). New York: Bantam Books.

Jensen, A. (1998, April). *Building a role model.* EQ Today web site. Available: www.eqtoday.com/jpcw98.html.

Steinem, G. (1992). *Revolution from within: A book of self-esteem* (pp.153–157). Boston: Little Brown.

Next Steps:
Increasing Your Capacity to Become More Self-Aware

Now that we've introduced you to the theory of self-awareness and what it can mean in an after-school setting, you might be wondering how you can start including these ideas in your own life and your own center or program. Making these ideas practical is an important part of *Bringing Yourself to Work*. Beginning with this chapter, we provide a guide of next steps to increase your capacity to *Bring Yourself to Work*—quick, easy things that you can do immediately to start the process of change for yourself, with your coworkers, and with the children in your care. In addition, we have developed a training program that will help you implement changes. Visit our web site (www.bringingyourselftowork.com) for more information about ways that you and your after-school program can get involved.

1. WRITE IT DOWN

Create a *Bringing Yourself to Work* journal. Divide the journal into three sections—one for self-awareness, one for relationship-building, and one for group relations. Keep the journal in a convenient place so you can jot ideas down quickly.

Why keep a *Bringing Yourself to Work* journal? A large part of increasing your emotional intelligence rests on becoming more aware—of your moods, and of things that trigger your emotions or make you unusually happy or anxious. You may want to know when are your most and least productive times of the day. Writing in a journal lets you recognize what affects the way you deal with children and staff at your center.

By writing down interesting, revealing, or noteworthy moments in your day, your journal will become a valuable resource to increasing your awareness of yourself, your relationships, and your role within your workplace.

Helpful tips

- If possible, write things down as soon as they happen. If you have a 5-minute break and you know of an entry you'd like to make, do it then.

- Try to commit a time each day or each week to write in your journal. Take that time to reflect on your day or week, and to think of observations to note in the three different sections.

- Look for deliberate opportunities for possible entries for your journal throughout your day. For example, try beginning your morning by looking for three positive instances of caregiver-child interaction to note in the self-awareness section of your journal.

- Be as specific and detailed as possible. If you felt awkward at a group meeting, for example, write down why. What was going on? If someone did or said something that made you feel uncomfortable, what was it?

- Don't feel you have to know why things happened in order to write down what happened. Sometimes starting with what occurred helps you figure out why at a later time.

- Be honest. No one is going to read your journal except you. Let your journal be the place that you note both what you do well and areas you know you can improve.

2. GETTING TO KNOW YOU

In the self-awareness section of your journal, make two columns on one sheet of paper by drawing a line down the center of the page. On one side, write down three unique talents or interests that you possess. Are you a good photographer? Painter? Soccer player? Are you interested in traveling to foreign countries? Arts and crafts? Gardening? Do you have a special knack for storytelling? Being a good friend? Active listening?

For each of the talents or interests you identify, brainstorm three different ways you could bring it to work. Think of some particular ways you could bring your passions to work, and write them down in the column on the opposite side of the page. Then figure out ways to make them happen.

- If you love traveling or multicultural awareness and diversity is important to you, could you organize an International Day at the center?

- If you're fascinated with animals, could you bring books on different animals into your program? Could you bring in your own pet or invite a local veterinarian for a show-and-tell kind of event?

- If music is your passion, could you have a day where you invite members of your choir to perform for the kids, and have the kids make their own instruments and perform as a group?

3. DEVELOPING YOUR EMOTIONAL INTELLIGENCE

Once you have read the following poem, try and answer the questions that follow.

Autobiography in Five Short Chapters by Portia Nelson

CHAPTER ONE

I walk down the street.
There is a deep hole in the sidewalk.
I fall in.
I am lost   I am helpless.
It isn't my fault.
It takes forever to find a way out.

CHAPTER TWO

I walk down the same street.
There is a deep hole in the sidewalk.
I pretend I don't see it.
I fall in again.
I can't believe I'm in the same place;
But it isn't my fault
It still takes a long time to get out.

CHAPTER THREE

I walk down the same street.
There is a deep hole in the sidewalk.
I *see* it there.
I still fall in . . . it's a habit . . . but,
My eyes are open.
I know where I am.
It is *my* fault.
I get out immediately.

CHAPTER FOUR

I walk down the same street.
There is a deep hole in the sidewalk.
I walk around it.

CHAPTER FIVE

I walk down another street.[3]

Questions

- What was the single thing the person in *Autobiography in Five Short Chapters* did to change her experience?

- How can a person's experience change if she accepts responsibility for what happens to her?

Think about experiences you've had that challenged you.

- Did you take responsibility for the part you played?
- Did you learn from the experiences?
- What lessons did you learn that you applied to future experiences?
- Are there times that you might have been better off if you had found another street to walk down?
- Are there some lessons that take longer to learn?
- Are you willing to be patient and work through the self-awareness process?

4. REFLECTING BACK

Think back to when you were a child and how you responded to change.

- Did you move to different homes a lot as a child?
- Did you change schools?
- Did a friend move away?
- Did your parents get divorced or remarried?
- Did the way you responded to change as a child differ from the way you responded to change as a teenager? From the way you respond to change as an adult?

As you reflect back on changes in your childhood, record your thoughts and your feelings. What emotions come up for you? Create a drawing or painting that represents what you know about yourself and change. You may want to ask a colleague to do the same and share your pictures with each other.

What have you learned as a result of reflecting back on change?

5. THE PROCESS OF CHANGE

Choose a recent experience that challenged you and one you would have preferred to have a different outcome. For example, you were at work and the director assigned a task to a colleague that you would have liked to do yourself.

Follow the 10 steps below, keeping in mind the recent experience you identified. Most people find it helpful to write down their responses. If you need some help, check out the example following the model.

A Problem-Solving Model

Step 1   *Problem*: Briefly describe the problem/situation.

Step 2   *Feelings*: Identify the feelings you experience when you think about the problem.

Step 3   *Body Scan*: Notice where in your body you experience the feelings.

Step 4   *Usual Response*: Describe what you usually do when you feel this way.

Step 5   *Satisfaction with Response*: Determine whether you are satisfied with your response.

Step 6   *Preferred Response*: If you are not satisfied, how would you prefer to respond?

Step 7   *Obstacles to Preferred Response*: Identify the obstacles that are in the way to responding the way you would prefer.

Step 8   *Worst/Best Fantasies if I Changed to my Preferred Response*: Identify worst and best possibilities. What is the worst thing that could happen if you responded the way you preferred? Don't stop at one—keep asking yourself, "So *then* what would happen?" At some point, your responses will start sounding a bit silly or unrealistic, and much of your worry may seem unfounded as you listen to how unrealistic some of your worst fears may be. Then ask yourself, what is the best thing that could happen if you responded the way you preferred?

Step 9   *Restatement*: Restate the preferred response.

Step 10 *Review*: Review and reflect the process you just went through. Notice whether you experienced any change in feelings. What did you learn? Can the learning be applied to other situations?

Example

1. *Problem*: I have trouble telling people what I want. I keep evaluating all of the ways to say it or ask for what I want, but then I don't follow through with any of them. One example of this is that I am always the staff person who goes outside with the children while my coworkers stay inside. I want to stay inside some of the time.

2. *Feelings*: Frustrated, worried, fearful, resentful.

3. *Body Scan*: Tightness in my chest, bad feeling in the pit of my stomach.

4. *Usual Response*: I say nothing. I continue to go outside and resent it.

5. *Satisfaction with Response*: Unsatisfied.

6. *Preferred Response*: I want to be able to express my preferences.

7. *Obstacles to Preferred Response*: I'm worried my coworkers will be angry or annoyed with me. I'm concerned they'll think I'm not flexible. I am uncomfortable speaking up.

8. *Worst Fantasies if I Changed to my Preferred Response*:

> They'll be angry with me.
> So what?
> I won't be liked.
> So what?
> I'll feel left out.
> So what?
> I won't want to go to work.
> So what?
> I'll lose my job.

As soon as it starts sounding unreasonable—that is, your preferred response of staying inside with the kids some of the time is very unlikely to lead to job termination—you may have begun to shift your thinking. You may come to realize how our fears can get in the way of taking action and making positive change.

Best Possibilities if I Express my Preferred Response:

> I get to be inside.
> I expressed what I wanted, and I feel good about myself.
> I discovered that no one really cared if I was inside some of the time.
> I felt closer to my coworkers because I no longer carried any resentments.

9. *Restatement*: I want to be able to express my preferences.

10. *Review and Reflect*: I feel better about myself and my coworkers. I learned that I don't have to be so afraid to express my views or preferences. Even if I didn't get to work inside some of the time, I still think I would feel good about myself for saying what I wanted.

This model for change is something that needs to be practiced often in order to become second nature. At first it may feel awkward, but in time, it will help you through the complex process of changing.

Building Relationships

Model for Change

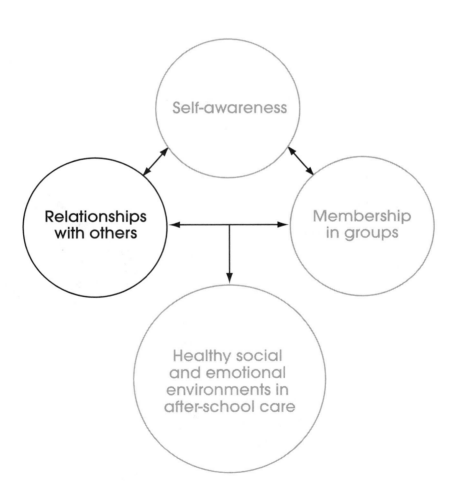

Self-awareness

Relationships
with others

Membership
in groups

Healthy social
and emotional
environments in
after-school care

> The ability to relate and to connect, sometimes in odd and yet striking fashion, lies at the very heart of any creative use of the mind, no matter in what field or discipline.
>
> —George J. Seidel

THE IMPORTANCE OF RELATIONSHIPS AND CONNECTION

As human beings, we have a fundamental need to be with each other, to share our experiences, to discover things about each other, to laugh, to debate, to play, and to connect. Whether it's a lifelong friendship with a classmate from elementary school or a daily ritual with the elderly man who sells coffee, the exchanges we have with people throughout our lives are extremely important.

The movie *Castaway* shows an interesting fictional example of the importance of being in relationships. In the movie, Tom Hanks's character survives a FedEx plane crash and washes up on the shore of a deserted island surrounded by a number of unopened FedEx packages. He is without food, drinking water, or any of the comforts of home, and he is totally alone. His need to talk to someone, to relate to someone—to *anyone*—is so great that he creates a friend out of a volleyball (something he found in one of the packages) by giving it a name, and decorating it with hair and a face. Throughout the movie, he totes the volleyball wherever he goes. He tells stories to it, cries with it, and even risks his life to "save" it after it floats away from his life raft. On that island, he needed desperately to connect with someone.

Take a moment to think about all the time and effort we put into forming and continuing relationships, from staying in touch via long-distance phone calls, letters, or e-mail to catching up with friends and family over a weekly cup of coffee, dinner, or a walk around the neighborhood. Even the momentary connections we make every day are opportunities for relationships—stopping by the bagel store before going to work in the morning and chatting with the counter person about our families; seeing a neighbor and spending a few moments finding out what's new before rushing off to work.

And although the desire to connect with other human beings is something we may share, our personalities and styles for building those relationships can be very different.

WHAT IS RELATIONAL ABILITY?

As we discussed in the previous chapter, self-awareness refers to your ability to understand your emotions and behavior. Being self-aware means being able to identify how you're feeling and behaving during your day. It also means being able to understand, on a very basic level, who you are, including what makes you tick, what your special talents are, and perhaps some behaviors you might want to change.

Just as people have different levels of self-awareness, they also have differences in *relational ability*. Relational ability refers to a certain set of skills—everything from being a good listener to speaking honestly about your feelings—that enables people to get along well with others. Although a person's relational ability also depends somewhat on his or her personality—outgoing people often have an easier time talking to others while shy or introverted people may find it easier talking to one person at a time—building meaningful relationships with others is something that can be learned and improved over time. Some people might be naturally drawn to social situations and others might be quieter. There may be times for the more outgoing person to sit back and observe, and the quieter person to engage and express her point of view. We all have the capacity to expand and change, and to develop new skills over our lifetime.

What do those skills look like? People with a high relational ability often know how to talk with other people; they know how to be supportive, caring, and

Case Study:
Relational Awareness at Wings for kids®

On Fridays, Wings for kids® sets aside a 40-minute period where each nest cleans, sweeps, or organizes a designated part of the school or its grounds. On one of the first Fridays of the school year, Alan Yarborough's nest of third-grade boys, the Falcons, was in charge of tidying up the courtyard—and it was going very badly. The boys were running amok in the courtyard—exactly the opposite of what they were supposed to be doing. The "ringleader" of the chaos appeared to be Davis, an 8-year-old boy in the Falcons with a history of behavioral issues.

"After the episode in the courtyard, I began to notice how difficult Davis was to work with," says Alan. "He wouldn't sit down when he was asked, he would call people names, and he was just generally disrespectful."

When Davis's behavior disrupted the classes of the other Wings for kids® leaders, they often called on Alan to refocus Davis on the task at hand. For reasons unknown to Alan, Davis listened to him more than any other Wings for kids® leader—and that made Alan realize the incredible opportunity he had.

Seeing the positive influence he had made Alan realize that Davis's long-term behavior probably wouldn't improve without some special action on his part. Alan

respectful. They know when to tell a joke to pick up a friend's spirits; they might sense a problem even if no one has told them; or they may be able to tell if a person is feeling uncomfortable, anxious, or lonely. People with a high relational ability are also self-aware people. By understanding their own behavior and moods, people with a high level of self-awareness often know how their behavior and mood affects those around them.

Having a high or a low relational ability may influence the way you bond with your friends, children and other family members, and coworkers. It may determine how comfortable people feel with you, and whether they feel understood, valued, and respected by you. As a caregiver, having a high relational ability is particularly important. With it, caregivers can understand how to have a meaningful and positive impact on a child in their care.

During our research, we heard the story of Gabriella, a 13-year-old girl in Oregon who found an incredible friend and mentor at a 10-week after-school drama program. The program was led by Lisa, an exuberant 24-year-old woman who divided each weekly class into two parts. During the first half, the kids took part in a series of dramatic exercises during which they acted out different scenes and tried their hand at improvisation and scene-writing. During the second part of the class, the kids explored what they had learned from the day's exercises by writing in a journal. The journals were handed in at the end of every class, reviewed by Lisa, and returned to the kids during the following class.

---

needed to figure out how to use his personal strengths to build a relationship with a child so obviously in need of attention and guidance. He started with the most noticeable thing in his favor: his size. Standing over 6 feet tall and built like a linebacker, Alan looked like a force to be reckoned with. The back of his T-shirt said it all: *Large and in Charge.*

"I knew I walked a fine line with Davis," comments Alan. "Sometimes the right approach was to be really stern—to give him a 'look,' to use a commanding voice, and to let him know that certain behavior just wasn't acceptable. For that approach, being twice his size certainly helped."

But other times, when a softer attitude seemed more appropriate, Alan could show by his words, by the look in his eyes. "I

know a lot of men might not be in touch with their 'sensitive side,'" laughed Alan, "But that isn't me. I'm very comfortable letting kids know I like them, and I think they respond really well to that."

Alan has a wonderful sense of humor, and through his humor he connects well with Davis and the other Wings for kids® children. "I'm an enormous third grader at heart," admits Alan. "I watch cartoons, I play video games, and I'd pretty much do anything for a laugh." Case in point: Alan was the sitting duck in last year's carnival dunk tank; and this year kids happily took turns pelting him with water balloons. "I think, deep down, kids see that I'm a lot like them. That allows them to trust me more, and to see me as someone who really understands what it's like to be them."

During the first week, Lisa noticed that Gabriella seemed mature for her age, but she also seemed very frustrated and unsettled. She acted out occasionally, choosing not to participate in certain games, showing up late and being critical of the other kids' performances. Lisa found it difficult to connect with Gabriella during the program. With a room full of other kids who also needed her full attention, there never seemed to be enough time to engage Gabriella or to start building a friendship. And after a few unsuccessful attempts to engage Gabriella in a friendly discussion before or after class, Lisa picked up the fact that Gabriella seemed uncomfortable with face-to-face interaction. What Lisa looked for was a way to reach Gabriella and give her the extra attention she needed.

So she turned to Gabriella's journal. It started slowly, first by writing notes in the margin or at the top of the page. Sometimes Lisa commented on something Gabriella had written; sometimes she asked questions about her day or other interests. Other times she wrote a paragraph or two about sharing the same feelings Gabriella had written about in one of her journal entries. They shared jokes; they discussed exercises that went well and others that needed some improvement; they swapped stories about being middle children and the siblings who drove them bonkers.

Gradually, the relationship between the two of them began to build. Each week, Gabriella would retrieve her journal and make her way to the back of the room to see what Lisa had written. In her final journal entry, Gabriella wrote that reading her journal became the most exciting part of her week. She admitted

His ability to empathize strongly with the kids in his nest brought about a huge turning point in his relationship with Davis. During homework time, a 45-minute period where each nest comes together with their senior Wings for kids® leader to work on unfinished schoolwork, Alan noticed that Davis was frequently disruptive.

The rule is, once the kids finish their work, they can read a book or draw," explained Alan. "Davis would just never pick up a book. He might draw, but only for a few minutes until he got bored or distracted. If he heard a voice outside the doors, he'd sprint to the window to see who was there, or he'd start talking really loudly to one of the kids across the room. So I began to think about what helped me focus and stay in my seat at that age."

And that's when Alan and Davis started playing checkers. "It wasn't part of the plan, but it was a really good idea. First of all, it allowed the other kids to finish their work without being interrupted, and it also gave the two of us time to talk about whatever was going on in our lives."

The topics changed daily—from Pokémon to sports to their home lives—but the result was the same: Davis stayed in his seat and the two developed a friendship that directly influenced Davis's behavior.

"He was much better behaved after that," says Alan. "He certainly wasn't perfect, but he really started listening more. He was calmer and the name-calling stopped almost completely. He would also come up and hug me for no reason. For a kid who couldn't even be touched at the beginning of the year, that was a huge deal."

Among all the moving and inspirational relationships we witnessed at Wings for kids®, we chose the story of Alan and

opening up to an adult in a way she never thought she would—even asking for advice and admitting that she often felt angry and alone. It was wonderful to write down her feelings and to be responded to with interest and caring. Lisa was keeping track of Gabriella, remembering her. And Gabriella was feeling *known*. Someone was interested enough in her to remember and to respond. Lisa shared how important the journal conversations were for her, too. She enjoyed getting to know Gabriella better. By taking the time to form a connection, Lisa made the effort to reach Gabriella by finding a vehicle—the journal. When one avenue didn't work, she kept trying and found another. There isn't just one way—you keep trying to find a way to connect with a person. Gabriella and Lisa created a relationship that neither one of them had expected.

MAKING A CONNECTION

In *The Healing Connection*, Jean Baker Miller and Irene Pierce Stiver suggest that moments of connection between two people, such as the one between Lisa and Gabriella, can lead to a relationship where both people feel valued and respected.[1] These moments of connection can be with someone you've known for years, such as a close friend, a relative, or someone you work with—almost anyone who might have spent meaningful time with you, listening to your successes or teaching you something valuable about life.

Davis for a few reasons. First, it effectively illustrates the theory described in Chapters 2 and 3. For example, one of the first things Alan did to build a connection with Davis was to become more self-aware. He asked himself what he was good at, what specific tools he possessed that could help him work more effectively with a child with behavioral issues. After coming up with three key things in his favor—his size, his sensitive nature, and his sense of humor—he used all three at different points in their relationship to build trust, closeness, and respect.

We also chose this story because the connection between Alan and Davis exhibits each of the five characteristics of a healthy relationship. In their discussions, Alan was *engaged* and *respectful* with Davis. Not only did he listen to Davis's stories about his friends or his favorite songs, but Alan shared some important details of his own life, such as the fact that he was an only child or that his favorite movie was *The Blues Brothers*.

Their relationship was *mutual*—they both learned from and enjoyed each other—and their relationship was also *authentic*. Alan was every bit himself during their relationship—goofy sometimes, stern other times—but always himself. But it was likely Alan's sense of *empathy*, his ability to put himself in Davis's shoes and remember what it was like to be an active 8-year-old that allowed the two to really connect. The idea to play checkers came from Alan's empathetic realization that if he were a restless and talkative young boy, playing a game might be the only way to keep him in his seat.

A moment of connection can also be just that, a brief but powerful moment that positively impacts one or both people. Think about a time when you found someone—maybe at a party, at a conference, or at work—with whom you truly connected. The two of you might have talked nonstop, exchanging stories, laughing, and finding out about one another. You may have explored your common ground and discovered you experienced similar things during your adolescence or during your marriage. You may have shared a story about losing your job or surviving a divorce that inspired and encouraged the other person. You may have listened as someone told you about being a single parent on her own for the first time, and how through that experience and its challenges she discovered she was capable of many more things than she could have imagined, a story that gave you a new perspective on raising a family.

A number of things can happen during those moments of connection. We often feel understood and valued, because not only was someone interested in hearing our opinions and experiences, but also shared his or hers. The experience makes us feel less isolated and alone. Knowing that someone else feels the same way we do—whether it's liking the same movies or hating being outside on the playground in cold weather—can make life easier or more enjoyable. Strong moments of connection also give us an incredible opportunity to learn more about ourselves and each other through the experiences of another person. Listening to a friend's story of her weeklong camping trip, for example, might awaken a sense of adventure in yourself. Hearing how a person responded to a challenging after-school situation may encourage you to explore what you might have done in a similar situation.

Whatever the circumstances, a moment of connection is a moment of discovery, comfort, and understanding between you and another person. It can be with a total stranger or with someone you've known since you were 5 years old. It can be brief or it can last a lifetime, and it can change the way we see ourselves and the people around us.

Just ask Elise, an urban schoolteacher of children with special needs. After a number of years in the classroom, Elise had started to question why she got into teaching at all. The daily challenges she faced in the classroom were taking their toll. At one time she was open, patient, and giving; now, she was short-tempered and impatient and had less and less energy to deal with the constant barrage of children acting out in her classroom. It had gotten to the point where she didn't like the person she had become.

One day, a colleague asked Elise if she could help with a computer lab at the after-school program located in the school. Elise wondered why she would want to spend any more time with children once the school bell rang, but a voice inside told her to say yes. Once there, she immediately noticed there was a different energy in the program than what she had been feeling in her own classroom. Beginning with the coordinator and flowing through to the other personnel and children in the program, this was a place where people shared not only their energy and creativity, but something more. The something more was an essential connection they seemed to have with themselves and one another. Elise saw children who were able to be vulnerable and open, trusting and curious, shy and caring. "These were kids who came from different countries and different experiences, but they were able to connect through laughter, sharing a sense of accomplishment, and working together," she says. "The joking, laughing, and sense of adventure began to have an effect on me as well."

Elise realized that being available to the children, relating to them, and establishing a sense of connection was just as important as anything she may have taught them about computers. She also realized that she needed the connection with them just as much as they needed to connect with her and with each other. They reminded her of why she enjoys teaching; of the gifts she has to give; and what sustains her each and every day. Now, she's reinvigorated and has brought the learning from her after-school experience to her regular classroom.

THE BENEFITS OF CONNECTION

Some of the most important research on the benefits of connection has come from Jean Baker Miller, Irene Pierce Stiver, and their colleagues at the Stone Center at Wellesley College. In their book *The Healing Connection*, Miller and Stiver explore how people's connections with their family members, colleagues, friends, and therapists can dramatically influence their psychological health. By drawing on their own experiences as therapists, the authors explore how deep and powerful connections with other people can help us grow and develop as human beings, while *disconnections*, the absence of connection, can lead to many psychological problems, including anxiety and depression. Meaningful connections, they believe, are a valuable and necessary part of human development for both men and women at every stage in their lives. And the research backs them up.

According to Daniel Stern, author of *The Interpersonal World of the Infant*, babies have an even greater innate ability to connect with their caregivers than previously thought.[2] As more and more research on infant mental health suggests, building relationships with other people is something we are born to do. The interplay between the mother or other caregiver and a child is the very first interactive dyad. The infant should be seen as a primary "self" who actively reaches to the mother—the establishment of the relational self, which is an early and real achievement. It's not a merging or symbiotic thing, as previously thought, but rather, these early experiences are experiences of being with someone.

The development of this early relationship between mother or other caregiver and baby sets the stage for later relationships. It affects the relationships of school-age children with caregivers, and later in life, relationships of adults with other adults.

Bridget

As Bridget Laird discovered, sometimes caregivers can have a profound impact on a child and not even know it. "Being the full-time director of Wings for kids® means I don't lead homework centers or choice time classes or spend as much time with the kids as I did last year when I was a senior leader," explains Bridget. "And I started wondering if I was still having an impact, if kids still felt close to me and considered me a friend." She didn't wonder for long. One afternoon, a fifth-grade boy named Tamik pulled Bridget aside and quietly asked to speak with her. "I could tell that he wanted to talk about something important. At first, he sort of skirted around the issue, but eventually I understood that he was nervous about going to a new school in the fall. He wanted advice and reassurance, and I was so happy he decided to talk with me."

In 1997, the *Journal of the American Medical Association* reported on a 2-year, $24-million study of more than 12,000 adolescents. The study found that teenagers with at least one strong adult relationship had the best chance of being healthy and avoiding high-risk behaviors, such as crime, drug use, and pregnancy. The study also discovered that the strong adult didn't need to be a parent or family member and could include a caring and nurturing role model from the teenager's church, community, or school.[3] Research from the national nonprofit organization Public/Private Ventures also highlights the positive effects of these mentoring relationships, including improvements in the youths' grades, school attendance, and the prevention of drug and alcohol initiation.

Another valuable study was conducted by Emmy Werner, an internationally recognized developmental psychologist who spent her life studying how children cope when confronted with adversity. Her study in the *American Journal of Orthopsychiatry* followed individuals from birth until age 32 and found that an established bond with at least one caregiver was the best indicator of health at age 18.[4] Again, this caregiver didn't need to be a parent and could include grandparents, older siblings, and neighbors.

If we know that moments of connection and stable relationships are the building blocks of emotional health, how can we identify ways to create these meaningful connections with other people, including the staff and children in our after-school program? What do healthy relationships look like, and how can we learn to develop more of them in our lives, both inside and outside the care environment?

WHAT DO HEALTHY RELATIONSHIPS LOOK LIKE?

Miller, Stiver, and their colleagues at the Stone Center at Wellesley College have identified the following characteristics that are present in healthy relationships.[5]

Authenticity

Moments of true connection start with being honest. If we think of the example of Lisa, the after-school caregiver at the 10-week drama program, and her student Gabriella, we can see how true this is. Their relationship took a dramatic step forward when both Lisa and Gabriella began sharing honest, emotional details of their lives with each other. Gabriella admitted feeling angry and alone, and Lisa shared a time when she felt the same way. By taking a small risk and writing a few notes in the margin of Gabriella's journal, Lisa helped pave the way for Gabriella to write how she truly felt, creating a relationship where something very special began to grow.

Respect

What if you told someone you were afraid of the dark, heights, or scary movies and they laughed at you? What if you knew that telling someone you were a Democrat, Jewish, or gay would mean losing that friendship? What if you knew that someone wouldn't like you or respect you because of your race? Healthy relationships are ones in which both people feel valued and respected, not just for their similarities, but for all the ways in which they're different. Respecting someone means being sensitive to another person's feelings and appreciating diversity on all levels, including differences in income, race, education, political affiliation, and sexual orientation, just to name a few.

Engagement

We've all experienced moments of engagement, when we really feel connected to another person. Neither of you are distracted; both of you are asking questions and listening closely. The conversation is cooking, things are moving along, and both of you feel like you have an equal opportunity to speak and to listen. Now think about a time when the opposite was true, when you had a conversation in which the other person wasn't paying attention. She might have been looking off in the distance, making a grocery list in her head, or was not in the mood to discuss this particular topic. You might have asked her a question, and she didn't respond. Or you might have had something important to share, but the other person kept interrupting, or began talking about himself. Whatever the circumstances, a connection can only take place when both people are present and participating.

Jeremiah

"When one of the kids in my classes acts up, I've learned to think about how they're feeling and to understand the environment they came from. Instead of sending them to the 'Peace Place,' where someone else figures out what's wrong or how to make it better, I know that's part of my responsibility as a Wings for kids® leader. I need to talk with the kids, to listen to them and not to give up on them."

Empathy

As we mentioned in the previous chapter, understanding how *you* feel about a situation or event might help you understand how other people would feel in a similar situation. This ability to put yourself in someone else's shoes, also known as empathy, is an important part of a successful relationship. As a caregiver, imagine a child who told you he was afraid to walk by the coat closet. He was certain that monsters lived in-between the shoes and jackets, and that one would surely pull him inside when no one was looking. He tells you that his heart is beating quickly, that he can't catch his breath, and that he's afraid to open the coat closet door. What would you say to this child?

There are countless different ways to respond, including telling the child he's being silly, or opening the cloakroom doors to prove that monsters don't really live inside. Unfortunately, neither of these responses is particularly sensitive. A more empathetic caregiver might try a different approach, one that focuses less on contradicting the child and making him "wrong" and more on sharing with him. Rather than telling the child he has nothing to be afraid of, or that monsters don't really exist, you might explain that being afraid of the cloakroom is something you can understand. Remembering her own childhood fears, one caregiver explained that when she was his age, she used to leap onto her bed from 5 feet away. She was convinced a monster lived underneath her bed and that he would grab her ankles if she got too close. By sharing that story, by showing him that other people understand how he's feeling, the child might feel better. The monster may still exist in his mind, but knowing that someone else has shared the same fear may make him feel less alone, less fearful, and more willing to share his feelings in the future.

Mutuality

Authenticity, respect, engagement, and empathy—four of the five essential ingredients of a healthy, meaningful relationship—hinge on the fifth ingredient:

namely mutuality. Relationships are a two-way street, and experiencing a true connection means that feelings and attention are going both ways, back and forth between the people involved. In other words, there is mutuality.

Why is mutuality so important? Because a meaningful connection is difficult to have when one person cares more about the relationship than the other. Think back to a friendship or relationship you may have had where one of you gave more time, more energy, or more of yourself than the other. Those are difficult situations, often because one person tends to feel needy, insignificant, or unappreciated. In cases like that, mutuality is not present.

An example of mutuality can be found in the relationship between Lisa and Gabriella. By writing back and forth in the journal, Lisa and Gabriella both shared personal details about feeling insecure and angry at different points in their lives. Within their relationship, respect, engagement, authenticity, and empathy were present on both ends—and that's what allowed them to connect.

Another example of mutuality can also be found between two caregivers. Imagine if another caregiver told you that he's having a bad day. He tells you that his sister, who was diagnosed with cancer, has been receiving radiation treatments that are making her very sick. It's been difficult for this caregiver to concentrate at work, he tells you, and he needs someone to talk to. As you listen to his story, you're engaged. You ask him questions about his sister's health and how his family is coping. You ask if there is anything you can do to lighten his workload. By honoring his request to keep this private, you're also being respectful. Perhaps you decide to share a story about your father's recent heart surgery, and how scary that was for you. As you describe that difficult time, you're being empathetic and authentic. By telling him about a real moment in your life, you're putting yourself in his shoes and trying to get a deeper understanding of how he's feeling.

The result is a connection that benefits both people. Each person is taking time to fully listen to the other. They're learning things about another person, and as they do, they're learning and exploring new things about themselves. Throughout their conversations, both people feel needed, valued, and respected. That's mutuality.

THE OPPOSITE OF CONNECTION: DISCONNECTION

Now that we've identified the characteristics of a meaningful connection, we should also spend a few moments examining what the opposite looks like: the moments of *disconnection* that prevent people from learning from one another and growing.

Disconnection is a moment of emotional or psychological separation from another person. It's a moment where someone feels cut off from the person they're with, as though they're not being understood or they're not understanding the

Keiron

"Children are not miniature adults, and that means they react differently than us. Things that might not seem like a big deal to us are earth-shattering for them. You've got to be aware of how they might see the world and be sensitive to those differences."

other person. If a relationship is a two-way street, a disconnection is like a giant stop sign or detour in the middle of the road. The conversation may grind to a halt or veer off in another direction because, in essence, the two people just aren't following the same path.

Disconnections can be minor or severe, ranging from a friend who looks distracted or bored during your conversation to a more complicated, more hurtful disconnection with a parent or a spouse.

A colleague once told us about an interesting pattern of disconnection between herself and her mother. When she was about 9 years old, Dana noticed that her mother, Nora, was often scattered and inattentive during many of their conversations. If Dana was in the middle of answering her mother's question or telling a story, Nora would often break into a story of her own or interrupt with a minor housekeeping matter, such as Dana's brother's pending dentist appointment. Each time, Dana would wait for her mother to resume paying attention before she continued her story. Sometimes her mother would apologize for interrupting and ask Dana to continue. Other times she forgot that Dana had been talking at all.

These experiences of disconnection were difficult for Dana, not only because they weakened her relationship with her mother, but also because they made it difficult for her to connect with other people in her life. She told us how she became jumpy and hypersensitive in conversations with colleagues, friends, or strangers. If she sensed that someone wasn't engaged or respectful—two of the five ingredients of a successful connection—she often became rude and defensive. The anger she felt at being ignored and disconnected at a young age carried over into her adult life, and her relationships suffered as a result.

The good news is that, eventually, Dana grew increasingly dissatisfied with her behavior and the mediocre relationships in her life. Remembering how she awkwardly waited to finish her stories at the dinner table encouraged Dana to become an engaged and attentive listener, one who always let other people finish their thoughts. Even in a group setting when someone was cut off mid-sentence, Dana would continue looking at the original speaker, undistracted by the new conversation, until that person finished. She knew how jarring and disruptive disconnection could be—not just the painful disconnection with a parent, but also the awkward disconnections between acquaintances in casual conversations.

HOW POWER CAN CAUSE DISCONNECTIONS

A disconnection can take place when any of the five ingredients of a healthy connection—authenticity, respect, engagement, empathy, and mutuality—are absent. That means for every disconnection, there are countless reasons why the disconnection might have occurred. Sometimes the explanation is simple. In the middle of your conversation, your friend remembered she has to pick up her daughter in 10 minutes, and looked at her watch so she wouldn't be late. A student who believes her opinions aren't worth sharing may have difficulty speaking up and being authentic. A caregiver who hasn't been exposed to other cultures may not be respectful or open to diversity. Other times, the explanation is more complicated.

Disconnections often occur in relationships when one person has power over another person. Think about how frequently disconnections occur in a family environment between children and their parents. In these cases, parents almost always have power over their children, which may make it difficult for both the child or the parents to be truly authentic. Kids might not be eager to share their experiences about sex, alcohol, or drugs with their parents because they believe there's a good chance they'll be punished. They might try to hide their grades, the dent in the family car, or the note from their teacher for fear that, if their parents knew the truth, they would be disappointed or angry. Parents wield a considerable amount of power over their children, both emotional and financial, and children know that.

Just as kids may have a difficult time being honest with their parents, parents may have an equally tough time sharing important and meaningful details about their own lives with their children. They may never tell the story of skipping school or being fired from a job, because the stories seem inappropriate or embarrassing. They might think that sharing the mistakes they've made will diminish their authority with their children.

How often have you heard children speak about their parents or guardians as though they were never kids themselves, as though they were born at the age of 30 or 40 having never experienced adolescence? "They don't know what I'm going through. They don't know what it's like. They were never a kid." It's often difficult for children to appreciate what their parents have lived through if those stories are never shared. As we mentioned earlier, those moments are more difficult to share, and it's harder to have a mutual and authentic connection when one person's desire to maintain power over another prevents her from sharing her true self.

Disconnections due to an imbalance in power are not limited to family situations; in fact, they exist in almost any relationship where one person has more power than another, including relationships between supervisors and coworkers, and between caregivers and children. During our research, we witnessed a powerful moment of disconnection as a caregiver led a group of children in a series of basketball exercises. In the middle of one of the drills, a young girl walked away from the games and sat in the bleachers, alone. The caregiver called to her from the middle of the gym floor, telling her to return to her place in line, but the girl refused. She sat in the bleachers, with the basketball beside her, and started crying. The caregiver did not ask her why she stopped playing in the game or why she was crying.

As the games continued, the caregiver approached the young girl and firmly told her that, unless she returned to the game and stopped crying, he and the rest of the children were going to ignore her. The girl cried harder, the staff person continued to ignore her, and no connection was made.

We all know how this situation could have turned out differently. A more relationally aware caregiver might have sat quietly with the girl for a moment, asking if she wanted to participate in the game and listening to her reasons for being upset. Rather than being a moment where two equals came together, where both people felt comfortable sharing how they felt, the situation looked more like a power struggle between a caregiver who demanded the exercise run his way and a young girl who, for whatever reason, did not want to follow the same schedule. In scenarios like this, caregivers have an enormous amount of power, which may make it difficult for a child to be honest about how he or she is feeling. Perhaps the girl felt awkward and uncoordinated. Maybe she didn't feel well, or she needed some time by herself. Perhaps the other children were teasing her. Whatever the circumstances, a moment of connection is difficult to have if one of the people (the child, in this case) doesn't have the opportunity to be honest or feel respected because she feels powerless.

The lesson here is that, even though caregivers will always be in a position of authority, where they have the power to make rules and to discipline children in their program, caregivers can also *share* that power so that both children and caregivers feel empowered. What if the caregiver had asked how the young girl was feeling or why she was crying only to discover that the issue was relatively minor? A few words of encouragement or a few moments of special attention might have been all she needed. By sharing her feelings in an environment where she felt safe and respected, the girl might view her caregiver as an advocate, as someone who is truly interested in her well-being. She might realize that she and her caregiver aren't on opposite teams—where he has all the power and she has none—but that they're on the same team. Sitting in the bleachers, the two of them could have talked through the causes for the girl's distress and worked out a solution so that they both felt respected, and listened to.

It's not always easy, but the power in an after-school environment can be shared. Doing so might mean asking children to choose that afternoon's activity, or involving them in the creation of the center's rules on acceptable behavior.

Sharing the power also means that caregivers are less interested in being "right" or in winning, and more interested in having an open dialogue where both have a chance to listen and hear. Through honest and empathetic discussions, caregivers help children find their voice and encourage them to use it to share their feelings and experiences with someone who is doing the same.

THE *CONNECTORS*: PEOPLE WITH A GIFT FOR BUILDING RELATIONSHIPS

In the beginning of this chapter, we introduced the concept of relational ability—the set of skills that determines how well a person connects with other people in his or her life. Throughout the chapter, we've also highlighted a few people with a high level of relational ability, those self-aware individuals who understand how their moods and behavior affect others, and who know the importance of things such as mutuality, empathy, and respect. We call those people *connectors.*

Think about a moment when you, as a caregiver, made a meaningful connection with a child. What did that look like? You were probably facing one another and making eye contact; you might have also made physical contact, such as a touch on the hand or shoulder. You were listening and being listened to. Empathy, engagement, respect, and authenticity were traveling back and forth between you. On an emotional and spiritual level, you reached out to a child and that child responded. There was a link between the two of you, like a cord that attaches to both of you. You were connected.

We've talked about the importance of being self-aware and the need to employ the five characteristics of a healthy relationship: authenticity, respect, engagement, empathy, and mutuality. Connectors are often people who have had good connections with others in the past, and who strive to create those connections again. These are people who are aware of their role as mentors, who know of the potential power imbalance between themselves and the children in their care. Connectors believe in helping to empower children, which helps them grow as individuals. Connectors also understand the risk of disconnection, and watch for opportunities to give children what they need to feel valued and respected.

But what are some other traits of these caring connectors who build exceptional relationships with children? During our research, we saw them in a variety of settings—in play groups, reading circles, athletic games, and one-on-one with children. By observing them in action and through interviews, we believe connectors are caregivers who

- View the children they work with as young people with promise, with unique histories, and valuable experiences
- Search for the special qualities in each of the children in their care
- Give generous amounts of attention and support to the children in their care
- Provide children with ample guidance and constructive feedback

In addition, connectors

- Are honest with themselves and with others
- Share details about their lives with people around them
- Reserve judgment and respect differences between themselves and others
- Believe in their own ability to make a difference in the world
- Feel they are giving something back to a specific community or to the larger society

THE FIVE GOOD THINGS

As we noted in Chapter 1, Jean Baker Miller says that five good things in growth-fostering relationships happen as a result of connection with another person: zest, action, knowledge, self-worth, and a desire for more connection. These same five good things are achievable in after-school programs, too.

1. *Zest.* There's a noticeable energy when two people truly come together. A sense of zest and vitality is present in after-school programs that place a high value on connection. These programs recognize the energy that comes from engaging children in a mutual, cooperative way. Children who are involved in planning activities, who feel heard when offering suggestions and ideas, respond with a sense of purpose and energy that's different from the other alternative—being told what to do.

2. *Action.* In one center we visited, the group—staff and participants alike—had developed a social contract, an agreement that guided how all members of the center would treat one another. The whole group worked on the contract together, and they constantly refer back to it as they strive to create the environment within the center they want. The effort demands constant attention from everyone involved, and concentrated action.

3. *Knowledge.* Having a more accurate picture of yourself and the others to whom you're connected comes from honest and open communication. Mutual respect flows from knowing your own particular strengths and vulnerabilities and those of your colleagues. Effective program administrators know this and create opportunities for staff to interact and learn each other's life stories.

4. *Sense of worth.* Developing a sense of worth is difficult (if not impossible) unless the people closest to you value your feelings and experiences. In centers across the country self-aware caregivers understand the power of language and signals and the vital role they play in making the children in

their care feel valued and heard. It means taking that extra few seconds to listen, to engage the child, and to value the moment of that exchange.

5. *Desire for more connection.* When four of the benefits of connection come together—zest, action, knowledge, and self-worth—so does the fifth: a desire to have more connection. Why? Because when you have a meaningful discussion with someone and experience an increase in your self-worth, a greater appreciation for the feelings of another person, a sense of participation and control, and greater energy and vitality, why wouldn't you want more opportunities to repeat this—and to create an environment where the kids are eager to connect with you and with others.

FOR FURTHER READING

Jordan, J. V. (1986). *The meaning of mutuality.* (Report No. 2)(pp. 1–11). Wellesley, MA: Stone Center, Wellesley College.

Herrera, C., Sipe, C. L., & McClanahan, W. S. (2000, April). *Mentoring school-age children: Relationship development in community-based and school-based programs* (pp. 8–12). Philadelphia: Public/Private Ventures. Available on-line: http://www.ppv.org/content/reports/mentreldev.html.

Miller, J. B. (1986). *What do we mean by relationships?* (Rep. No. 22)(pp. 1–12). Wellesley, MA: Stone Center, Wellesley College.

Miller, J. B. & Stiver, I. P. (1997). *The healing connection: How women form relationships in therapy and in life* (pp. 24–41, 49–52). Boston: Beacon Press.

Resnick, M. D., & Bearman, P. S. (1997). Protecting adolescents from harm: Findings from the national longitudinal study on adolescent health. *Journal of the American Medical Association, 278*(10), 823–832.

Spencer, R. (2000, August). *Relationships that empower children for life: A report to the Stone Center directors* (pp. 15–17). Wellesley, MA: Stone Center of the Wellesley Centers for Women.

Stern, D. (1985). *The interpersonal world of the infant: A view from psychoanalysis and developmental psychology.* New York: Basic Books.

Surrey, J. (1985). *The "self-in-relation": A theory of women's development.* (Rep. No. 13)(pp. 1–10). Wellesley, MA: Stone Center, Wellesley College.

Werner, E. E. (1989). High risk children in young adulthood: A longitudinal study from birth to 32 years. *American Journal of Orthopsychiatry, 59*(1), 72–81.

Next Steps:
Increasing Your Capacity to Be in Relationships with Others

WRITE IT DOWN

In your journal, write down an example of a time when you experienced a moment of connection—times when you felt that you and the person with whom you were speaking were truly engaged, respectful, empathetic, and authentic. Try to be specific, recording why you feel that a particular conversation or exchange was different from others you've had. Why did you feel understood or valued? Why did you feel better after the conversation? What happened that you would like to see happen again?

GIVE AND GET

One of the most essential skills in building effective bonds with others, particularly in a child-care setting, is being able to *give and receive constructive feedback*.

Think of all the times when you, as a caregiver, guide the behavior of children in your program. Whether it's teaching them not to throw things at each other or explaining the benefits of sharing, much of your job involves shaping their behavior in more positive, constructive ways. That can also be true of your relationship with other staff members, whether you're offering suggestions on organizing the supply closet or planning a sports day. Giving constructive feedback is just one way many people try to improve their program.

EFFECTIVE INTERPERSONAL COMMUNICATIONS

The quality of our relationships with others is often dependent upon the quality of our communications. Effective communications is comprised of two components: sending messages and receiving messages—or speaking and listening.

Review the following tips for sending and receiving effective messages. Identify those items you do well most of the time. Identify those items you believe need improvement. Improvement comes from practice. You can practice interpersonal communications every time you interact with someone—your partner, a colleague, a child, a relative, a friend. You may find it easier first to practice with people with whom you're comfortable, then apply your skills to more difficult relationships.

- Own the message. Use "I" or "my" rather than "some people" or "the group." For example, you might say "I have some concerns about the schedule," instead of "Some people think there is a problem with the schedule." Using "I" statements helps you take responsibility for your own actions.

- Make your message clear and specific. Give the listener all of the information she needs to completely understand you. Find out where she is in her understanding, and start there. Use words she can understand.

- Make what you say and how you say it match. More than 90% of communication is nonverbal. Does your body language match what you're saying? A person is more likely to believe the way you say something than the words you use to say it. Tone of voice is important as well.

- Focus on what is most important. A listener can only hear and remember a certain amount of information. Tell him the most important information first.

- Focus on the positive. Look for areas where you agree as a common place to begin. Building trust between you and your listener will help when you have difficult issues later on.

- Choose a time that's good for both of you. Ask the other person if it's a good time to start a conversation or a discussion, especially if there is any conflict. If not, set a future time so that both of you will feel you have enough time to express yourselves fully.

- Be respectful. There are always two sides to every story and two points of view. Don't make assumptions about what the other person's view is or what his or her motivation may be.

- Ask for feedback about the way your message is being received. Check on how the other person is receiving what you're saying. Check for understanding and how he or she feels about the content. Ask, for example, "Does this make sense to you?"

- Name your feelings. To do this effectively, start your sentence with "I feel . . ." and be specific about the feeling. Many people say, "I think . . .", which isn't as personal. Sharing your feelings by name is a good way to develop rapport between people.

- Agree to disagree. It isn't always possible to come to agreement. Once you both thoroughly understand the issues and the other person's point of view, you may choose to respectfully disagree—with the ideas rather than with the person.

- Be empathetic. Put yourself in the other person's shoes and try to see the issues from her perspective.

- Be as effective a listener as you are a speaker. Paraphrase what you hear to ensure you have understood it. Don't interrupt. If you're interrupting, it's a sign that you're thinking more about what you're going to say than what the other person is saying.
- Listen with all of your senses, not just your ears. Watch for nonverbal cues as well.
- Be curious. The best listeners are interested in what they are hearing.
- Ask questions. Good listening produces questions. Ask for more detail. Explore what is being said.
- Suspend judgment and take on more of an observing role. Listening requires openness. You cannot be open if you make judgements about what is being said.

Effective communication is the basis for a healthy relationship. To determine if you are a good communicator, score yourself on the following questions, with a score of "1" being hardly at all and "5" being most of the time.

1. When speaking, I clarify, restate, and summarize important points.

   1   2   3   4   5

2. When listening, I make eye contact and nod as a way to show I understand.

   1   2   3   4   5

3. In conversations, I let the other person finish before I speak.

   1   2   3   4   5

4. I ask follow-up questions to clarify what is being said.

   1   2   3   4   5

5. When responding, I stay on the other person's topic rather than moving the conversation to other topics.

   1   2   3   4   5

Total your score and multiply by four. A score of 60 or below indicates there is significant room to improve your interpersonal-communication skills. A score of 61 to 79 indicates there is some room to improve your skills. A score of 80 or above indicates you are an effective communicator. Keep practicing your skills.

Healthy Relationship Indicators

As Jean Baker Miller notes, whenever we're in a healthy relationship, five good things happen:

1. *Zest*—a noticeable energy that's created as a result of two people truly coming together
2. *Action*—a willingness to take steps necessary to continue the relationship
3. *Knowledge*—a willingness and openness to learn about the other person
4. *Sense of worth*—the development of a greater sense of self-worth as a result of being in the relationship
5. *Desire for more connection*—the desire to have more: more zest, action, knowledge, and self-worth

Think about the relationships you're in. Select one particular relationship in each of the following categories:

- A family member
- A friend
- A working colleague
- A child in your program

For each of these relationships, take each of the five healthy relationships indicators and describe in your journal how the relationship provides, or doesn't provide, the particular element. Then for each relationship, answer the following questions:

- Is this a healthy or an unhealthy relationship?
- Are there enough healthy indicators in this relationship to continue working on it?
- If so, what could I do to improve this relationship?
- What would I need to ask of the other person to improve the relationship?
- What have I learned as a result of being in this relationship?
- What elements of this relationship would I like to take to other relationships I have?

The capacity to connect with others is instrumental in developing yourself fully. Ask yourself, "What can I do to connect more with this person in my life?"

Chapter Four

Being a Member of a Group

Model for Change

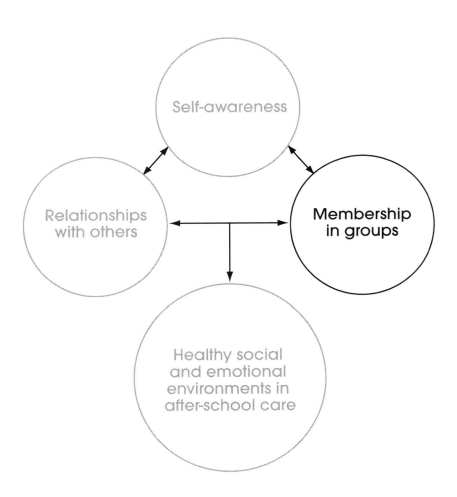

Self-awareness

Relationships
with others

**Membership
in groups**

Healthy social
and emotional
environments in
after-school care

None of us is as smart as all of us

—Japanese proverb

YOUR ROLE AS A TEAM MEMBER

Whether or not you watched the television series *Survivor*, you're probably familiar with the show's premise. Sixteen strangers are divided into two teams, stranded in a remote location with minimal supplies, and pitted against one another for food rewards, the right to stay in the game, and in the end, a million-dollar jackpot. The show was a broadcasting phenomenon and generated millions of coffee-break conversations in workplaces across the country.

Besides being entertaining, *Survivor* got millions of people talking about *group dynamics*, our topic for this chapter. Episode after episode, viewers painstakingly assessed the motives and behavior of the individual group members: is he lazy, is she bossy, is he strong enough, is she a good leader? They also analyzed the performance of each team as a whole. They noticed how some *Survivor* teams operated like well-oiled machines, while others were plagued with gossip, backbiting, and disorganization. What's interesting is how the group dynamics were always changing.

As the contestant makeup changed throughout the game—as people came and went—the groups' energy and productivity shifted. Sometimes they were more effective, sometimes less. For example, some teams found their groove once a certain member was voted out of the game. Once that person was gone, the energy changed. There was less negativity, less competition, more harmony. In other cases, the loss of a particular member hurt the team significantly. Maybe that person was a leader, a motivator, a supporter. Whatever their role, their presence was missed. The group just wasn't the same without them.

What many of us recognized while watching that program was how profoundly each individual team member can affect the performance of a group. He or she can be a burden or a benefit, a help or a hindrance. And not just on *Survivor*—in any group, including an after-school team.

Take a moment to think about the kind of group member you are. Are you a positive force within your team, or a negative force? Do you participate in group discussions, or do you tend to hang back? If you see a way to improve your program, can you present your ideas clearly and persuasively? Are you usually enthusiastic about change in your program, or do you dread it? Are you normally a leader? A cheerleader? A naysayer? A gossip?

In order to build on both your self-awareness and relational awareness discussed in Chapters 2 and 3, this chapter deals with the third arm of our model for change: understanding how you function as part of a team. That means examining the attitudes and behavior you bring to a group, how that behavior impacts the rest of your team, and whether you're leading your group closer to or further away from its goal of creating a happy, healthy learning environment for children and staff.

WE'RE ALL IN THIS TOGETHER

It seems like an obvious point that you, as an after-school caregiver, are a member of a group. After all, you're not at your job alone. You're part of a team that usually includes a director and other caregivers, all of whom perform various functions within your program. Some people handle administrative tasks; some people work with children; some people plan activities; some people perform multiple tasks within the group. Whatever their individual roles, the staff works together as a team.

Case Study:
Group Relations at Wings for kids®

During the first year of Wings for kids®, the kids and staff organized a truly special activity. On a sunny spring day, in the concrete and grassy courtyard behind the school, the group held a carnival. Everywhere you turned, there were exciting games, hot food, and kids running in every possible direction. The event was a smashing success—one that couldn't have been done without teamwork.

One year later, when the time came to plan the carnival again, the senior staff knew that a successful event depended on the participation of the entire Wings for kids® community. That meant involving the volunteer caregivers in the initial planning sessions. How could they get the children involved? How would they earn tickets? Who would work the booths? When would clean up time begin? Together, the caregivers met with the Wings for kids® director, Bridget Laird, to offer suggestions and to troubleshoot. No idea was a bad idea; no concern was too small to discuss.

"We really wanted to do this as a team," says Bridget. "To have a really successful carnival, people needed to feel like they helped put it together—not just the Wings for kids® leaders, but the kids, too."

Getting the children involved started weeks before the actual event. The first step? A brainstorming session where the

There is a certain routine to being part of an after-school team. You have meetings, planning sessions, and general discussions on how to manage your program. You might gather in groups to discuss a troubling incident that happened earlier that day—perhaps a child who consistently gets into fights—and you work to understand how to help that young person. Together, you may have to deal with a number of unexpected challenges, such as the dismissal of a staff member, a sudden drop in enrollment, or a change in location. Whatever the circumstances, being an after-school caregiver means working with a group of people to manage day-to-day operations.

This isn't always easy. As many of us know, things can happen in groups that don't usually occur when just two or three people gather together. There's a different energy, different rules and, often, different challenges. Think about a meeting you attended where you noticed some of the different dynamics at play within your group. Perhaps you realized that some people weren't getting along, which made the meeting more tense than usual. Some people might have been goofing off or repeatedly interrupting, which dragged the meeting on forever. Perhaps two or three people were talking nonstop, which left other people in the meeting feeling silenced, as though their comments weren't welcome. Watch any group gathering and you'll see—there's a lot going on.

Given how complex group life can be, what explains why some groups work together better than others? Why are some after-school programs, for example,

kids planned the kind of booth they wanted, including the rules, the prizes, and the work schedule. Once the plans were made, and each nest had planned their booth, it was full steam ahead. The children were given daily updates on the status of the preparations, volunteers were enlisted, and the excitement began to build.

"After all the buildup and anticipation, the day of the carnival finally arrived," says Bridget. "And I think we were all surprised by the level of teamwork and commitment from both the kids and staff. There was a definite transformation in people, that's for sure."

One of those transformations involved the entire nest of senior Wings for kids® leader Alan Yarborough. "In the past, my nest hasn't worked well when they were unsupervised," says Alan. "But at the carnival, they were awesome. Some of the kids ran the water balloon booth while the others filled up balloons on the other side of the courtyard. I had visions of them goofing off, popping all the balloons and not getting anything done, but that wasn't the case. They took their role in the carnival very seriously and did exactly what they needed to have a great booth."

Bridget described another impressive transformation the day of the carnival, this time by a young girl overcome with enthusiasm to participate at her booth. "At one point during the carnival, while I was inside the school, I saw a young girl sprinting through the hallways. When I asked her to slow down, she breathlessly explained that her work shift was about to start and that she had to get to her booth *right away*.

more efficient, positive, or supportive than others? How did they get that way? Most important, how can you, as an individual member, help your group create the best possible environment for children and staff?

YOUR IMPACT ON THE GROUP

As we saw in the *Survivor* example, one of the keys to creating a successful group is understanding that you, as an individual, can have a profound impact on the way your group functions.

Try to think of relatively minor situations where your behavior might have affected the people you work with. For example, if you regularly leave after-snack cleanup to the last minute even though your colleagues plan to use the same tables for an art project when snack time is over, your behavior affects the amount of time available for the activity and creates resentment among the team members.

If you are a team leader or director, your responses influence the tone of the program and how much initiative people feel they can take. If you're usually critical of new ideas, are people hesitant to brainstorm with you? Could your group be more innovative or creative if your behavior was more supportive and accepting? Or is your leadership style so uncertain and hesitant that people don't know what is expected of them?

We bring a host of attitudes and experiences related to countless different issues to our workplace every day—everything from how we feel about authority

---

She was so focused and serious, it was amazing."

Organizing 120 children, 10 different booths, prizes, food, supplies, and cleanup is no small task. For Wings for kids®, what made the difference between a smooth event and one that was disorganized and halfhearted was having a solid group of team players behind it. In this chapter, we listed a number of traits of effective team members, almost all of which can be seen within the example of the Wings for kids® carnival.

First, every member of the Wings for kids® program was on board and working toward the same goal of having a fun-filled, successful carnival. To ensure that everyone felt involved, the staff created an open, respectful environment that per-

mitted other caregivers and children to suggest how to make the carnival even better. Caregivers listened to the children in their group, and were flexible in trying to work their suggestions into the event where possible.

As a group, the staff and caregivers showed an impressive amount of empathy. By putting themselves in the children's shoes, and figuring out what would make the carnival the most fun, a number of good ideas came up, such as asking the children to decide what kind of booths to create and finding a simple way for them to earn as many prize tickets as they could. Alan even agreed to be the target for his group's water balloon booth, saying he couldn't imagine anything the kids would enjoy more.

figures to how committed we feel to our workplace. We all have our own way of seeing things, and most important, each of us has different ways of reacting. If a staff member resents being told what to do, for example, he might repeatedly challenge the center's authority figure or not do what was asked. If someone doesn't plan on staying at the program for long, she may put less effort into doing the job well. If someone is insecure or inexperienced, he may feel hesitant taking on a leadership role, such as offering suggestions or mentoring other staff.

Each of these actions can directly impact the rest of the group. The person who constantly challenges the center's director might cause a considerable amount of friction within the group. A person who is consistently late or often absent will create more work for the rest of the team. A person who feels hesitant speaking up or offering suggestions could withhold valuable insights that might help the program run more efficiently. Depending on the actions of just one person, the level of harmony, tension, or productivity can change significantly within the group.

WHAT MAKES A GOOD TEAM MEMBER?

Just as people have varying degrees of emotional intelligence and relational ability, they also have varying skills as team members.

Throughout your life, you've probably noticed individuals who are extremely effective at motivating or communicating with other people. They usually have a certain mix of personality, intelligence, and experience that enables them to get

Examples of cooperation and collaboration were everywhere throughout the event—from caregivers who watched each other's booths to kids who completed tasks together, such as preparing the face-painting booth or creating the course for a 20-yard dash. Bridget Laird also told us an impressive story of bond-building between two children, one of whom had a stack of prize tickets while the other had very few. The child with more tickets promptly gave half of his tickets to his friend so, in his words, "they could both have fun."

Following the successful event, the Wings for kids® group met with the senior staff to debrief: What had gone well? What had surprised or impressed them? What hadn't gone well? And, given the group's constant desire to improve, how could they improve the event for next year? The kids also debriefed the event. What did they do well as a team, and in what ways could they have improved? What did they do well individually, and how could each of them have done things differently to make the event even better?

One consistent theme that emerged was participation. The caregivers noted that everyone felt involved in the event, especially the kids. There was a commitment from them that few had expected. This was *their* event, one caregiver commented, and it seemed to bring out the best in them.

along well with others, and the response is usually the same: people listen to them. People value their suggestions and act on what they say.

The good news is that, just like emotional intelligence and relational ability, the skills to become an effective group member can be learned. Great team members aren't just born that way—they've learned to be that way. In his book *Working with Emotional Intelligence*, Daniel Goleman lists three skills of effective team members that can be developed over time—building bonds, cooperating, and modeling teamwork.[1]

Building Bonds

During our research, we met Rosa, a bubbly, up-beat caregiver who is an excellent example of a "bond builder" within an after-school setting. At the time we visited, Rosa had worked for the after-school program for 8 months, and was the newest team member. Despite being new, she commanded a level of affection and support you might only expect for someone who had worked there for years. After watching her in action, it was easy to see why.

During our visits, Rosa routinely arrived at the center early to make coffee and chat with staff members as they began their day. The conversations ranged from movies they'd seen to work-related matters, but all of them were friendly and warm. During the day, Rosa frequently connected with other staff members by asking about their kids or their softball team or their vegetable garden. She would place thoughtful Post-it notes on people's In baskets, commenting when an activity had gone well. Staff members told us how generous Rosa was, both with her time and her possessions: she would lend books to people if they mentioned liking a particular author, she offered people rides home, and she acted as a professional and personal sounding board when people needed an empathetic ear.

Rosa's interest in others and her supportive nature did more than make her a well-liked member of the team. These qualities also set a certain tone for the other staff members. By regularly connecting with the rest of her group, Rosa was taking conscious steps to demonstrate the kind of behavior she'd like to see from the other caregivers. Given that she wanted to work in a friendly, open, and safe environment, she made sure to be as honest, considerate, and trustworthy as possible. In other words, Rosa was taking deliberate steps to create a group that was in sync with her values and attitudes so that she—and others—could bring their true selves to work.

Collaborating and Cooperating

People who are successful at building bonds know one important rule about thriving in a group: people are valuable resources. The more people you have connections with, the better. Why? Because someone might have important information you could learn from, or they might be able to lend a hand. Bonding with oth-

During her winter holiday break, Julie, a first-time Wings for kids® leader, made two important realizations: (1) The kids in her nest didn't follow the rules because she didn't enforce them and (2) she had been afraid to enforce the rules because she wanted the children to like her. She knew this needed to change.

Julie

During a few meetings with her entire nest, Julie took responsibility for how the group had been behaving. She told them the truth—that she was new at being a caregiver and that she wanted the kids to like her. And then she asked for their help in becoming a better leader.

The result? Not only did the children in her nest become a better behaved, more cohesive group in less than 2 months: they also understood that true leadership means being honest about your behavior and asking for help to improve it. "I learned that Julie's got a nice, soft heart and that we can't be mean to her," says 9-year-old Aleesha. "She taught us how to respect each other—and that's why we all get along now."

ers is a way to build a strong network of people, each of whom represents complementary knowledge, expertise, or support if you need it.

One of the benefits of strong work relationships is that people like Rosa receive support whenever they need it. In the spirit of collaboration and cooperation, her coworkers are more than willing to switch shifts, help her with an activity, or share their expertise. Rather than hoarding their special skills or protecting their own work time or agendas, Rosa's coworkers are eager to answer questions, offer input, and work cooperatively. An athletic coworker might enthusiastically help Rosa run the program's sports day, for example; or someone with a lifelong interest in Egypt may help shape her session on the ancient pyramids.

Whatever the circumstances, Rosa and her coworkers have created a cooperative, collaborative, and efficient team. They understand that pooling their resources creates a stronger, more knowledgeable group than if each of them worked in isolation. They've recognized a fundamental truth about business today: Each of us has only a fraction of the knowledge and experience it takes to do our jobs well. We need each other—and valuable team players know this.

Modeling Teamwork

As a caregiver, becoming a more valuable team member means modeling certain behavior in order to help your group get along, being motivated, and staying on track. The two skills described above—connecting and cooperating—are two of many. In his writings on teamwork, Daniel Goleman lists many more characteristics of good team members, such as being

- Self-aware
- Respectful and open to different opinions
- Empathetic
- An excellent listener
- Committed to the group's goal
- Flexible
- Driven to improve

In his research on automobile plants, technology firms, and pharmaceutical companies, Goleman shows how real the benefits of teamwork can be. Effective groups are usually more efficient and can often save large companies millions of dollars by completing projects on time and on budget. Flexible teams that work well together are also groups that feel safe sharing ideas and being creative—and that means they're often more inventive. Some products and solutions owe their very existence to solid teamwork. Without an open, trusting, and supportive environment, those ideas might never have seen the light of day.

The benefits of teamwork for after-school programs, although difficult to measure in dollars and cents, are just as real. Throughout our research, we saw programs where teamwork was high and, in some cases, where it was low. In one program—one that ranked very high on the teamwork scale—the individual staff members showed a high level of concern and support for one another.

At this program, we watched as a group of four staff members met to brainstorm strategies that one of them, Krista, could use in helping a particular child who seemed to need more attention and had a hard time joining the group during activities. One person suggested paying special attention to the child before an activity, and then immediately afterwards, making sure she felt a connection. Another suggested giving this child a defined role—handing out materials, writing on the board—to encourage her to participate in a constructive way.

Many of Goleman's elements of teamwork can be seen within this one example. Krista displayed a great deal of self-awareness by recognizing that she needed help in dealing with one of her kids. Rather than sticking with a strategy that wasn't working, Krista was flexible and asked her coworkers to help improve her approach. In the process, she listened to their suggestions and respected each person's opinions, even when they differed from her own.

Her coworkers were extremely empathetic—after all, they've all been in similar situations before. Each one of them remembers dealing with a challenging child—

> ## Charnequa
>
> "I noticed there was one very strong girl in my nest, who led—or tried to lead—most of our group activities. Once I realized that, I began to create opportunities so that all the kids could be leaders, whether that meant helping me at the front of the class, being the spokesperson for their group, or choosing our next activity."

how they wanted to help but how, after some unsuccessful attempts, they felt powerless to make a difference. Given their own experiences of needing assistance, combined with their commitment to producing happy, healthy children, they all pitched in to help Krista. Their teamwork not only created a solution for Krista's challenge; it also sent a message to the rest of the staff, old and new: This is a trustworthy, supportive team that works well together. This is a place where staff members can ask for help and offer help because, in the end, they want to be stronger as a team.

THE GROUP'S EFFECT ON YOU

As we described earlier, the first step to becoming a valuable team member is being self-aware and realizing that you, as an individual, can dramatically affect the way your group works. By building bonds and modeling team-friendly behavior, such as cooperation, empathy, and respect, you can help build an effective, energized team that works well together. You might only be one staff member among many, but your behavior can certainly have an impact.

But self-awareness is only part of the equation. In the end, making a valuable contribution within a group also means recognizing that groups, like people, have varying degrees of emotional intelligence. You could be the most emotionally intelligent person around, for example, but find yourself in a group that doesn't share the same skills or priorities. You might want to model some of the elements of teamwork listed earlier, but find that the group isn't receptive. How will this affect the self you bring to work?

As a member of any group, it's important to understand that just as you're part of a larger, interdependent system in which your behavior will influence the group, the group's behavior will also influence you. How does that happen? Each group has its own values and attitudes that may rub off on you, causing you to act in ways you otherwise wouldn't, for better or for worse. Depending on the group's dynamic—whether its level of emotional intelligence is high or low—your behavior might follow suit.

Before we examine how your behavior might be affected by the dynamic of your after-school group, let's look at the kind of group to which you belong. What does it look like, how does it operate, and where do you fit in?

LOOKING AT YOUR GROUP

Take a moment to examine your after-school program as a group. What are its goals and habits? Is there a lot of interaction, or do people usually keep to themselves? What is your role within the organization? Do you feel valued? Do you feel comfortable offering input at staff meetings? How does your group normally get things done? If organization or efficiency starts to slide, how does it get back on track? Is there a lot of complaining about the administration of the director instead of honest dialogue about what feels wrong? Do staff accept responsibility when things don't go well? Do people scapegoat each other?

As you're assessing your group's dynamic, try thinking about it in terms of the categories Malcolm Knowles identifies in his book *Introduction to Group Dynamics*: goals, norms, atmosphere, cohesion, and structure.[2]

Goals

What is your group's reason for being? Why does it exist? Is it to make money, to give people jobs, or is the goal broader than that? If the goal of your after-school program is to inspire children and staff, to provide them with the best social and educational opportunities available, ask yourself if everyone is on board. Does the whole team share that vision, and what might happen if everyone doesn't?

Norms

Whether they're spoken or unspoken, every group sets a standard for acceptable behavior that can influence how the individual members behave. These standards, or norms, can govern the acceptability of everything from interrupting people to borrowing supplies to calling in sick. What are some of the norms of your group? Is it typical for people to finger-point or blame others when times are tough or things go wrong? Do people routinely clean up after each other, or does one person do it all? What are the "rules" of your group?

Cohesion

Have you ever walked into a room and felt like your presence wasn't wanted? Maybe you, the newcomer, sensed that the "old timers" at your job didn't accept

> **Chris**
>
> "Part of being a good leader is recognizing that change won't happen overnight. You may want to see results right away—like better behavior or a better group dynamic—but behavior and attitudes take time to change. You have to be patient."

you. They might not ask your opinion or include you in their conversations. Or perhaps you've had the opposite experience, where you've been welcomed openly by a group. Perhaps people took the time to introduce themselves and make you feel like you belong. Where does your group fall on the cohesion scale: Is it friendly and open, or cool and distant?

Atmosphere

Atmosphere describes the mood or climate of a group. It might be difficult to define, but it's often very easy to sense. A warm, friendly, and relaxed atmosphere is very different from one that's tense, antagonistic, and cold. What is the atmosphere like in your after-school program?

Structure

Structure refers to the way a group is organized, how decisions are made, and who has authority in the group. Some groups are open and flexible, while others are more closed, less flexible. In one group, questioning a director's decision might be welcomed; in another, the question might be ignored or have negative repercussions. Structure can determine how much input you, as an employee, are authorized to give. You might feel more valuable in an open, nonhierarchical group than in one that sets too many limits on how much you can contribute.

THINKING ABOUT GROUP DYNAMICS

It's important to know that groups have their own personalities, just like individuals. When you become a group member, your behavior can often be influenced by the group's personality, and the reverse is also true. To understand how, think about the following scenarios for a moment.

Jason is sitting with a number of his coworkers as they discuss how to handle a disciplinary issue with one of the children in the center. The group is divided right down the middle—half believe the boy should be asked to leave the program and half believe he should be given another chance. Throughout the discussion, three people in favor of asking the child to leave shout down anyone from the other side who tries to make a point. They cut people off, roll their eyes, and make stinging personal criticisms of anyone who disagrees with them. Nobody in the room does anything to steer the conversation out of their hands. Jason, one of the people who firmly believes the child should be given another chance, doesn't feel safe sharing his opinion with the group and remains silent.

Lynette, a recent college graduate, is offered a job with a young, dynamic after-school center. The director of the program enlists the help of her entire staff to set the organization's rules, goals, and curriculum. She encourages questions and discussions among the staff, and commends initiative. Lynette flourishes in this environment and develops a sense of leadership and responsibility she never had before. She begins to problem-solve and troubleshoot in ways she never thought she would, in part because the entire staff helped her develop the skills she needed to work well within this group.

Had Jason or Lynette been asked to describe themselves, they might have painted a very different picture than their behavior suggests. Jason may have described himself as vocal and argumentative. But within a group environment where the atmosphere is threatening or aggressive, his behavior may change.

The norms of this group may have prevented Jason from participating in the debate. If yelling and insulting people are permitted within this group, someone who prefers a more calm, respectful discussion—such as Jason—may opt out. The cohesion of this group is another factor affecting Jason's behavior. If this group were less threatening, Jason might feel comfortable asking his coworkers to stop making fun of people who disagree with them. If they were all friends, he might make a lighthearted comment to break the tension so everyone could participate. *Come on everyone, let's play nice. Okay people, no throwing things.* But this wasn't the case.

Jason did not participate in the discussion because he felt unsafe and bullied by some of his coworkers. Jason may be a very self-aware person—one who would normally speak up and share his opinion—but the dynamic within the group did not offer the safety he needed to bring his true self forward.

Similar things might be said for Lynette. She may have considered herself timid or irresponsible, but an experience with a helpful and emotionally intelligent group changed that. The group's norms included offering constructive advice, listening to each other, and lending a helping hand—norms that helped Lynette develop a sense of confidence and improve her skills as a caregiver. The group's structure was less rigid than it might have been in an older, more established after-school program. The group's flexible, energetic director made sure to include all the caregivers in shaping the program. As a result, Lynette was making a positive contribution to her program, and she knew it. She felt valued and appreciated, something she had never experienced at a job before. In addition, the group's supportive atmosphere and sense of cohesion also positively influenced Lynette's behavior and enabled her to recognize intellectual and personal resources she didn't know she had.

Understanding how you normally behave during an argument, in times of stress, encouragement, or confrontation is only half the equation. Knowing that you're usually talkative, collaborative, patient, or honest in your day-to-day relationships is important, but it may not accurately predict how you'll behave in certain groups. Why? Because when you're part of a team, there's something else that may curb or influence your own personality—namely, the group's own dynamic.

WHAT ARE THE CHARACTERISTICS OF A SUCCESSFUL AFTER-SCHOOL GROUP?

From our research in the field, and our own experiences raising and working with children, there's one thing we know for certain: creating a healthy social and emotional environment for children and staff doesn't happen by accident. It takes work.

Part of that work involves being self-aware and recognizing the behavior you bring to your program every day. It also includes assessing your group's dynamics and examining the factors that might change the way you normally behave. The next step is to think about the kind of group you want to belong to, and then to model behavior that matches your ideal.

If you want to work where you're free to take risks, for example, then you'll want to help make it safe for other people to take risks. That might mean reserving judgment if someone makes a mistake or supporting a coworker when he is trying something new. If you want to work in an open, honest environment, you'll want to be open and honest yourself. That might mean speaking up when something bothers you or listening to others when they have suggestions or concerns about their work environment. If you want to work in an environment that recognizes creativity and hard work, you'll look for opportunities to acknowledge other staff members for their contribution. If someone planned a great activity or handled a challenging situation with confidence and flair, you'll want to tell her. Why? Because doing so encourages the kind of behavior that makes learning and working together much more rewarding.

So what kind of behavior do effective after-school groups display? What kind of group dynamics offer the best chance for creating a socially and emotionally healthy learning environment for kids? What kind of behavior should you as a caregiver be modeling and working toward as a member of a group? Based on our experience and research, we've identified a list of characteristics of successful, emotionally intelligent after-school environments.

Emotional Safety

These after-school programs provide honest, respectful, and emotionally safe environments where staff members look out for your well-being. In an environment like this, you could tell a coworker you're having a bad day and expect support and understanding, not repercussions. Gossiping and back-stabbing are not acceptable group norms. People feel comfortable asking for help when they need it. In a safe environment, everyone can be himself or herself because there are genuine feelings of acceptance and support among the group members.

Caring

People are friendly and social in these groups. In a caring environment, there is humor and a genuine interest in other people's lives. If one of the group members had exciting weekend plans, members of the staff will ask for details on Monday morning. There is a curiosity in these environments. *Is your cold better? Is there anything you want to talk about? Can we as a group do something to make things easier for you today?* In a caring environment, members of a group realize they're working as a team. When one of its members wants to share an exciting story or express frustration or sadness, other members of the group are there to listen. Why? Because they realize they may need similar support in the future and because, ultimately, caring about each other makes their group stronger.

Sensitivity

Successful after-school programs often have a "listening environment," where people's suggestions, concerns, fears, and preferences are heard and respected. If someone has a problem, people take it seriously. They listen, they take responsibility for any role they play in the problem, and they find ways to make things better. In a sensitive environment, people are empathetic. If someone is tired or stressed out, they try to imagine how they would feel and act accordingly. They might give the other person a break from what he or she is doing or offer some other show of support.

Opportunities

A healthy after-school environment offers you the opportunity to be creative, and to learn more about yourself, your work, other people, and the world around you. It's an environment that supports each person's abilities and offers guidance when indicated. People aren't left to succeed or fail on their own. People who are strong in one area often mentor other staff members and, in turn, are mentored in an area they want to develop. In an environment like this, there are opportunities for people to grow and change. The director and other staff members give each other permission to take risks, try new things, and bring forward fresh ideas. In this environment people are recognized and rewarded for hard work and dedication.

Leadership

In these organizations, everyone in the center feels comfortable assuming a leadership role. They know that a leader isn't someone in an ivory tower who hands down decisions from above. Members of these groups realize that a leader is anyone who helps strengthen relationships within the group or who moves the group toward its goals. As a result, everyone seizes opportunities to offer suggestions or help their group operate more efficiently. Members of these groups care about staff morale and look for ways to improve it. In an open environment such as this, people feel inspired to make a difference because they've been given permission to do so.

Personal Responsibility

A healthy after-school program promotes the responsibility of its members to shape their experience within their group. Members don't rely on other people to solve problems within the group; instead they look at what they can do to make changes and improve things. Rather than pointing fingers or looking for a scapegoat, members of these groups take responsibility for their own behavior. If the sporting equipment isn't put away properly, they don't blame the director for not showing them how. Instead, they make sure they ask how the equipment should be put away so they can do it properly next time. If people are consistently late for meetings, they don't blame the traffic. Instead, they learn to leave their house earlier. The result is a group of people who know that having a successful after-school program starts with them.

Vision

A functional group also has a very clear vision of what they want to do and how they want to behave. Do they want to endorse yelling at meetings or gossiping behind people's backs, or do they want to promote calm, friendly meetings and honest, forthright discussions? A group with vision also passionately moves toward the goal of establishing the best possible environment for children and staff. They ask themselves: How can we prepare kids to be caring participants in the world? How can we give them the tools they'll need to be happy, productive citizens in the community? In other words, they ask if they're doing everything they can to help children and staff grow and develop as human beings.

YOU AND YOUR GROUP: FINDING THE RIGHT FIT

A great deal of this chapter has focused on what you, as an individual caregiver, can do to improve the social and emotional climate of your after-school program. We've talked about how building a successful center starts with you, and how each of your actions—procrastination, organization, negativity, efficiency, pettiness—can cause a chain reaction within a group. We did this to draw attention to the influence that just one individual can have on a number of people working together.

Having said that, it's also important to recognize that your behavior may have less impact on your team than you might have hoped. In some groups, modeling emotionally intelligent, team-friendly behavior might be very rewarding. Children and staff might take a lesson from the positive behavior you bring to work, and change the way they deal with each other. They might become better listeners or better communicators. They might learn to share more, yell less, or work more efficiently. Slowly, you might see incredible transformations right before your eyes. Unfortunately, this might not be the case in every after-school group.

At some point in your life, you may join the staff of an after-school program with goals and norms that are very different from your own. You might want a relaxed atmosphere, but theirs is quite rigid. You might believe that all staff should have input into the center's curriculum and policies, but the director isn't open to that. You may want to be part of a "learning organization," constantly adding new skills to your resume through courses and learning from other staff members, but the center doesn't have the time or resources to help you along. What do you do then?

The answer is not always a simple one. In cases such as this, it's important to remember that you have a choice. You can either stay at that center, trying your best to bring your most honest, true self to work despite the differences, or you can find another program that's more in synch with your values and attitudes. Whatever decision you make, remember that there are some environments where you'll feel more comfortable bringing yourself to work than others. Wherever possible, try to find those programs. And while you're there, we encourage you to be as aware of *yourself*, your *relationships*, and your *team* as possible—because the end result is a more enjoyable experience for you, other staff members, and the children in your care.

FOR FURTHER READING

Banet, A., Jr., & Hayden, C. (1977). A Tavistock primer. In J. E. Jones & W. Pfeiffer (Eds.), *The 1977 annual handbook for group facilitators* (pp. 155–167). La Jolla, CA: University Associates.

Colman, A. D., & Bexton, W. H. (Eds.). (1975). *Group relations reader*. Sausalito, CA: GREX.

Goleman, D. (1998). *Working with emotional intelligence* (pp. 198–231). New York: Bantam Books.

Hirschhorn, L. (1997). *Reworking authority: Leading and following in the post-modern organization* (pp. 26–29). Cambridge, MA: MIT Press.

Hirschhorn, L. (1999). *The workplace within: Psychodynamics of organizational life*. Cambridge, MA: MIT Press.

Klein, E., Gabelnick, F., & Herr, P. (Eds.). (2000). *Dynamic consultation in a changing workplace*. Madison, CT: Psychosocial Press.

Knowles, M., & Knowles, H. (1969). *Understanding group behavior: An introduction to group dynamics* (pp. 1–12). New York: Association Press.

Next Steps:
Increasing Your Capacity to See Yourself as a Member of a Group

WRITE IT DOWN

At your next staff meeting, pay close attention to what is happening.

- How do people interact with each other?
- How do you interact with the other members of the staff?
- What kinds of emotions do people display at these meetings?
- What kind of emotions are you feeling and displaying?

It's important to be aware of the role you are playing and the roles other people play.

- Does someone take on the role of encouraging others to share their ideas?
- Does someone consistently block the ideas of others?

When you write in your journal, think about the various roles people play at your workplace. What role do you play? Most importantly, think about, and write down, how you feel as people play their roles. Writing down your feelings helps you better understand them.

ONE DAY AT A TIME

For one month, allot 1 day each week to develop the different skills you bring to the group. Choose things you know you are good at, as well as other skills you may need to work on. For example, every Monday you might intentionally look for opportunities to build bonds with other members of the staff. On Tuesday, you may concentrate on finding ways to cooperate and collaborate. (Refer to the chapter for other skills of effective group members.)

Write down your experiences, reflections, and thoughts in your journal. Try and capture the responses you may have received from other members of your group. The results will give you a sense of how you may impact the group, as well as where your individual actions had very little impact on how the group functioned.

RULES FOR CONSTRUCTIVE CONTROVERSY

All groups, at one time or another, need to make decisions. Many times, not everyone in the group can agree what the right decision should be. The following exercise will give you a sense of the skills required to take part in a group that has conflict or controversy, or which simply needs to make decisions.

Read the checklist below and put a check mark beside those items you do consistently, without much difficulty. Put an X beside those items you have difficulty with or would like to improve on. Make a list of those items beside which you placed an X. Next time you're in a group, practice to improve these areas. Evaluate your performance.

- I am critical of ideas, not of the people having them. When working with children, this is the same as separating the "deed" from the "doer."

- My goal is to come up with the best solution, not to win or to get everyone to agree with me. (The definition of a team is a group of individuals all "pulling" in the same direction.)

- I want everyone in the group to have a say and to take part.

- I listen to everyone's ideas thoroughly before stating my own. I don't interrupt as soon as I think I know what the person is going to say.

- If I don't understand what someone has said, I ask for clarification, in a nonthreatening way.

- I don't make my mind up until I've heard all sides of the issues.

- Even if I don't agree with ideas being offered, I try to understand them and make sense out of them.

- If I hear new information, I am willing to change my mind. I consider changing my mind, not an indication of being weak, but as being open to new ideas.

Improvement requires continual practice. Some people find it helpful to enroll friends and colleagues into their learning process. You can tell some of your coworkers, for example, the areas you'd like to improve in. Then, following the meeting, ask them to help evaluate your performance in the meeting.

Chapter Five

Making Change Happen in Your Progam

Model for Change

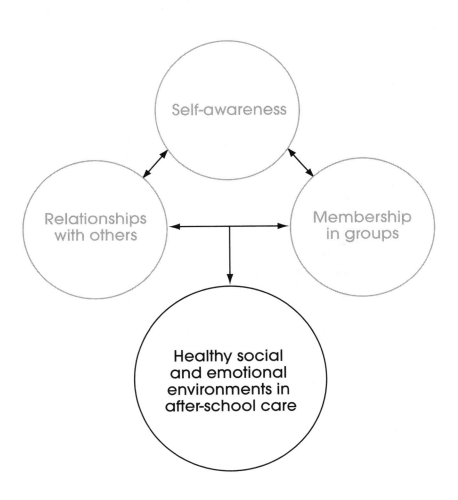

> The self is not something ready-made, but something in continuous formation through choice of action.
>
> —John Dewey

WORKING TO CHANGE

If you've gotten this far in our book, you will have learned new things about self-awareness, good relationships, and positive group experiences in after-school programs. The preceding chapters outlined in detail each of the three key components of our model for change in after-school programs:

- Becoming more self-aware
- Building stronger relationships with others
- Working more effectively as a member of a group

This model for change is based on the central idea that if you are able to create a culture within your center or program where staff are free to be who they are, to build trust and connections with others, and to work effectively as a group, you will create a healthy social and emotional learning environment where children can grow and thrive. We believe that whatever you have learned through this book and choose to apply will filter down to the children and youth in your program who learn by looking at you and emulating your behavior.

Through our research, we have seen programs where our ideas about training for after-school staff have come to life and the results are compelling. We visited a multicultural program that serves 40 adolescent girls in Massachusetts. Because relationships are central to the program structure, adults create and take advantage of opportunities to talk with the girls about personal matters, either one-on-one or in small groups. The adults share information about their own lives, passions, and interests. When staff break down the power dynamics that often exist between adults and youth, the teens can take a more active role in planning and implementing activities, and this kind of participation offers opportunities for social and emotional learning and growth. That's an example of "power with" rather than "power over," an important tenet of relational practice.

On the day we first visited this program, the staff and participants invited us to join their sharing circle. The activity often begins with a "body scan" where each participant directs her attention to feelings and tensions in her body and then shares those feelings with the group. The lack of hierarchy between staff and youth at these moments is remarkable, and the teens say that this sense of community makes them feel comfortable and supported in the program. Tanya, one of the participants, called the sharing circle her savior. She says it allows her to express herself, sometimes by crying, sometimes by side-splitting laughter. Whether she is laughing or in tears, she says that it always feels good.

Caren, one of the staff leaders, pointed out that because the girls are sensitive about feeling judged, the program staff tries to provide a sanctuary from the kinds of pressures they face with grades at school or performance in sports or with peers. Staff have been able to create this safe environment because they participate in their own sharing circles where they discuss memories of their own adolescence and issues that affect their capacity to help the girls. The adults learn to know themselves and each other as individuals with strengths and weaknesses, joys and troubles, before they interact with the youth in their care.

The girls are able to build relationships with the staff as well as with each other because they have learned how to share parts of their inner selves with the entire group, kids and staff alike. As Amy, one of the participants, says about the staff, "They don't have authority over us. It's not them and us—it's all *us*. They share what they are feeling and what's happening in their lives with us. It's nice to know that adults have feelings, too." This is a program driven by a clear understanding of the value of connection, safety, and trust, and you can feel it the second you walk in the door.

As this example shows, there are programs operating throughout the country today where self-awareness and connection are central to the program's mission. In these programs, the ideas presented in this book are not theories or abstract concepts; they are real, they are the fabric that binds these programs together, and they are making lasting impacts in the lives of caregivers and children alike. We also know from experience and observation that these ideas are applicable across all types of programs and can be adopted by any center, whether it's a homework club that places an emphasis on academics or a city recreation center that places an emphasis on physical activities. The content or mission of the program is not the issue. Rather, the philosophy of the program is. It simply means asking staff and administrators to reorient their compasses and place the emotional needs of the children at the top of their list of priorities. That is not an easy task. It means making changes in the way they're used to doing things and embracing ideas that may seem obvious and unfamiliar all at the same time.

Through the research and writing of this book, through holding training sessions with caregivers and others to introduce them to the practice of *Bringing Yourself to Work*, we have seen the power and potential of change. We have seen it at Wings for kids®, where Ginny Deerin realized she no longer wanted to "live her life small." That simple vision led her to create an entire program based on building relationships, and increasing her own self-awareness and the self-awareness of the staff and children who make up the program. Wings for kids® became a place where it is safe to make all this happen.

We have seen it in New York City where a schoolteacher named Elise, tired and frustrated by the tough conditions at her school, left herself open to the possibility and potential of helping the children in an after-school computer program and was rewarded in ways she could never have imagined. Rather than saying "no" when asked to volunteer for the program, Elise listened to her own inner voice, which reminded her that when she was a young girl, meaningful connections with her teachers were the life preservers she clung to as she made her way in the world. Taking a chance—making a change—revitalized Elise and reminded her why she began teaching in the first place.

So now what? How do you translate the ideas in this book into action? How do you decide that you'd like to do things differently? How do you know when you need to make some changes?

Changes like those Elise, Ginny, and others experience are not easy to come by. Change challenges people. It asks us to grow, to view the world differently, and to act in new and different ways. Oftentimes change is scary. Sometimes we feel as if every fiber in our body is being challenged and stretched, demanding something unique and special from ourselves. It also demands our full attention and the courage to face things that we may not wish to know.

We also know that it is much easier to talk about the desire to change than to actually take the steps to move in a different direction. No matter how uncomfortable we might be with our own behaviors, attitudes, and reactions, they are what is most familiar to us. We know ourselves best *as we are* and that provides a certain amount of comfort. But trying to change will almost always make a person feel *uncomfortable*—sometimes very uncomfortable. This might mean feeling awkward, out of sync within oneself, even artificial. This is a good thing, because when we feel out of sync or awkward, it means we are behaving in a new and unfamiliar way and that is where there are opportunities to grow and change. Think about making a change to get in shape if you haven't done any physical activity for a long time. The first time you go to the gym can be a nightmare. Maybe you don't know how all the machines work. You struggle to do the exercises or get winded after walking on the treadmill for only a few minutes. The next day your muscles are killing you. You feel uncomfortable, but after a few weeks of sticking to a routine, doing the hard work, you begin to see results. The aches and pains are a distant memory as you begin to lift more weight or start running instead of walking.

In the Preface, we captured this notion of conscious, intentional change by saying that "change is magical, not magic." We firmly believe that change can occur anytime and anywhere, but it requires a commitment to making the desired change happen. You know what it takes to make changes in your own life, whether it be changing your diet or trying to be more physically fit. That same conscious, intentional approach to change is required in an after-school setting. But the important thing to realize is that change can happen in many ways and can come from anywhere in an organization. It can happen in small steps, and it can start with you.

Following this chapter is a Self-Assessment Tool to help you rate your emotional intelligence. Going through this process can enable you to mobilize the strength and personal resources to take the first step on the road to change. The Tool is designed for an individual, but it can easily be adapted for use by a staff group.

THE NEXT STEP IS YOURS

Making change happen in your program is only possible if two essential ingredients are in place:

- Leaders in your program must want to engage in a change process. Without them it will be very difficult to shift your program's focus to an emotionally aware environment.
- Leadership is a state of mind. It starts with an internal feeling that you are able to make a positive difference in people's lives. It means seeing an opportunity to make your job better and grabbing it. It means showing an interest in becoming a better caregiver and learning how.

We realize that before you can act, you must believe in your own ability to change and to grow. Whether you're motivated by the examples in this book or by something in your own experience, we hope you see the enormous power one person can have in guiding, nurturing, and teaching another. We hope you realize your potential to make deep, meaningful connections based on trust and understanding with the coworkers and children in your lives.

We also hope that *Bringing Yourself to Work* can help you channel that power and potential in the best ways possible:

- To gain a better understanding of yourself and your relationships with others.
- To spot opportunities to extend a caring, knowledgeable, and supportive hand to the people in your life.
- To see that you can be a leader, and to experience that change is possible.

Ultimately, it all begins with you—as you act by *bringing yourself to work*.

Appendix

Self Assessment Tool

BRINGING
YOURSELF
TO WORK

The questions below relate to three main areas of emotional intelligence—self awareness (S), ability to relate with others (R), and ability to relate within a group setting (G)—and are labeled that way in the left margin.

Please take some time and be as honest as you can. Give yourself a higher rating if you both know the statement is true and you are able to behave that way the majority of time. Give yourself a lower rating if you recognize the statement as valid, but don't often behave in that way. For example, "When in a group, I share decision making with others." Perhaps you know sharing decision making is a good idea and you do it all the time. Or, you might believe it's a good idea and you strive to do it, but most of the time you find it difficult to share decision making.

The only person who will benefit from completing the questions is you, so being honest with yourself is a sure sign of emotional intelligence.

On a scale of one to five, with one being "Never" and five being "Always," circle the response that best captures your experience.

S 1. I know how I feel most of the time.
(Never) 1   2   3   4   5 (Always)

R 2. I treat others with respect, regardless of their age, sex, or relationship to me.
(Never) 1   2   3   4   5 (Always)

G 3. I believe that my behavior in a group setting can greatly impact the group.
(Never) 1   2   3   4   5 (Always)

S 4. I am aware of when I feel angry.
(Never) 1   2   3   4   5 (Always)

R 5. I believe that what I say can affect the people around me.
(Never) 1   2   3   4   5 (Always)

G 6. When in a group, I share decision-making with others.
(Never) 1   2   3   4   5 (Always)

S 7. I learn from past mistakes.
(Never) 1   2   3   4   5 (Always)

R 8. I believe that how I feel can impact the people around me.
(Never) 1   2   3   4   5 (Always)

G 9. I accept the differences between my work colleagues and myself.
(Never) 1   2   3   4   5 (Always)

S 10. I am aware of the impact I have on others.
(Never) 1   2   3   4   5 (Always)

R 11. I believe that people have the right to set limits, and I need to respect the limits they set for themselves.
(Never) 1   2   3   4   5 (Always)

G 12. I believe that groups make better decisions than individuals.
(Never) 1   2   3   4   5 (Always)

S 13. I am able to stay positive during difficult times.
(Never) 1   2   3   4   5 (Always)

R   14. I know the difference between relationships that are good for me and bad for me.

(Never) 1   2   3   4   5 (Always)

G   15. I am good at taking the lead in resolving conflict.

(Never) 1   2   3   4   5 (Always)

S   16. I can laugh at myself when I make mistakes or things don't turn out exactly as I planned.

(Never) 1   2   3   4   5 (Always)

R   17. I know when a work colleague and myself are not getting along with each other.

(Never) 1   2   3   4   5 (Always)

G   18. I can talk comfortably with others at work about topics we strongly disagree on.

(Never) 1   2   3   4   5 (Always)

S   19. I believe I can make a positive difference in the lives of others.

(Never) 1   2   3   4   5 (Always)

R   20. I recognize when someone is angry.

(Never) 1   2   3   4   5 (Always)

G   21. I am aware of the unofficial role I play in my work setting.

(Never) 1   2   3   4   5 (Always)

S   22. I feel comfortable at work expressing my feelings to others.

(Never) 1   2   3   4   5 (Always)

R   23. I can often sense a problem even though no one has talked about it.

(Never) 1   2   3   4   5 (Always)

G   24. I am aware of the impact my colleagues at work have on me.

(Never) 1   2   3   4   5 (Always)

S   25. I adapt to change easily.

(Never) 1   2   3   4   5 (Always)

R   26. I don't take on responsibility for people's feelings at work.

(Never) 1   2   3   4   5 (Always)

G   27. I am aware that I have an impact on my colleagues at work.

(Never) 1   2   3   4   5 (Always)

S   28. My own description of my personality characteristics closely match the way my work colleagues would describe me.

(Never) 1   2   3   4   5 (Always)

R   29. I have no difficulty talking with a colleague about issues we disagree on.

(Never) 1   2   3   4   5 (Always)

G   30. I can talk comfortably with friends about topics we strongly disagree on.

(Never) 1   2   3   4   5 (Always)

S   31. I feel comfortable at home expressing my feelings to others.

(Never) 1   2   3   4   5 (Always)

R   32. I easily let go of feelings I have resulting from arguments or disagreements with colleagues.

(Never) 1   2   3   4   5 (Always)

G   33. I can put myself in another person's shoes, even if I haven't experienced the same set of circumstances.

(Never) 1   2   3   4   5 (Always)

S 34. I am aware of the circumstances under which I feel happy.

(Never) 1   2   3   4   5 (Always)

R 35. I believe that people I work with will take my interests into consideration.

(Never) 1   2   3   4   5 (Always)

G 36. I am aware that everyone responds to things differently.

(Never) 1   2   3   4   5 (Always)

S 37. I can manage my emotions easily.

(Never) 1   2   3   4   5 (Always)

R 38. I trust my judgement of people's character.

(Never) 1   2   3   4   5 (Always)

G 39. I believe that people's past experiences affect the way they are today.

(Never) 1   2   3   4   5 (Always)

S 40. I am aware of the circumstances under which I feel sad.

(Never) 1   2   3   4   5 (Always)

R 41. I tell the truth even if I have difficult things to share.

(Never) 1   2   3   4   5 (Always)

G 42. I believe that my own past experiences affect and/or influence who I am today.

(Never) 1   2   3   4   5 (Always)

S 43. I know when I am tired.

(Never) 1   2   3   4   5 (Always)

R 44. It is easy for me to trust people who I work with.

(Never) 1   2   3   4   5 (Always)

G 45. I can influence and/or inspire people around me.

(Never) 1   2   3   4   5 (Always)

S 46. I take initiative to start new activities.

(Never) 1   2   3   4   5 (Always)

R 47. I take initiative in my relationships with others in my personal life.

(Never) 1   2   3   4   5 (Always)

G 48. I take initiative as a member of a group of colleagues at work.

(Never) 1   2   3   4   5 (Always)

Self-Assessment Scoring Key

Enter the number of your response (between one and five) in the space corresponding to the question. Then total your responses by adding down each column.

1. ___	2. ___	3. ___
4. ___	5. ___	6. ___
7. ___	8. ___	9. ___
10. ___	11. ___	12. ___
13. ___	14. ___	15. ___
16. ___	17. ___	18. ___
19. ___	20. ___	21. ___
22. ___	23. ___	24. ___
25. ___	26. ___	27. ___
28. ___	29. ___	30. ___
31. ___	32. ___	33. ___
34. ___	35. ___	36. ___
37. ___	38. ___	39. ___
40. ___	41. ___	42. ___
43. ___	44. ___	45. ___
46. ___	47. ___	48. ___
Totals ___	___	___

Your score

- The first column relates to self-awareness.
- The second column captures your ability to relate with others.
- The third column refers to your ability to relate within a group setting.

To determine your current ability to Bring Yourself to Work, focus on two things: your total score in each column, and how your scores in each column compare to each other.

A score of 70 to 80 in each column suggests you are doing an excellent job of Bringing Yourself to Work. A score of 65 to 69 suggests you are doing a very good job and there is some room to improve and learn more. A score of 60 to 64 suggests you are doing a good job, but there is still more to do. A score of below 60 in any one of the areas indicates an area where you want to concentrate some attention so you and the children in your care can have a fuller experience.

Notes

PREFACE

1. Goleman, D. (1997). *Emotional intelligence* (pp. 13–55). New York: Bantam Books.
2. Seppanen, P. S., et al. (1993). *National study of before and after school programs.* (Final report to the Office of Policy and Planning, U.S. Department of Education)(p.15). Portsmouth, NH: RMC Research Corporation.
3. Posner, J. K., & Vandell, D. L. (1994). Low-income children's after-school care: Are there beneficial effects of after-school programs? *Child Development, 65,* 440–456. Vandell, D., & Shumow, L. (1998, July). *Future of children.* Unpublished paper.
4. *Ibid.*
5. Resnick, M. D., & Bearman, P. S. (1997). Protecting adolescents from harm: Findings from the national longitudinal study on adolescent health. *Journal of the American Medical Association, 278*(10), 823–832.
6. Pianta, R. C. (1999). *Enhancing relationships between children and teachers* (p. 17). Washington, DC: American Psychology Association.
7. Goleman, D. (1998). *Working with emotional intelligence* (pp. 198–231). New York: Bantam Books.

CHAPTER 1: BRINGING YOURSELF TO WORK

1. Shonkoff, J. P., & Phillips, D. A. (Eds.). (2000). *From neurons to neighborhoods: The science of early child development* (pp. 315–317). Washington, DC: National Academy Press.
2. Spencer, R. (2000). *Relationships that empower children for life: A report to the Stone Center Directors* (pp. 15–17). Wellesley, MA: Stone Center of the Wellesley Centers for Women.
3. Goleman, D. (1997). *Emotional intelligence* (pp. 13–55). New York: Bantam Books.
4. Salovey, P., & Mayer, J. D. (1990). *Emotional intelligence: Imagination, cognition and personality* (pp. 9, 185–211). Weisinger, H. (1998). *Emotional intelligence at work.* San Francisco: Jossey-Bass. Seligman, M. (1991). *Learned optimism.* New York: Knopf.
5. Cohen, J. (1999). *Educating hearts and minds: Social emotional learning and the passage into adolescence* (pp. 3–20). New York: Teachers College Press.
6. Miller, J. B., & Stiver, I. P. (1997). *The healing connection: How women form relationships in therapy and in life.* Boston: Beacon Press.

7. Hirschhorn, L. (1999). *The workplace within: Psychodynamics of organizational life*. Cambridge, MA: MIT Press. The A. K. Rice Institute for the Study of Social Systems, P.O. Box 1776, Jupiter, FL 33468.

CHAPTER 2: BECOMING MORE SELF-AWARE

1. Goleman, D. (1997). *Emotional intelligence: Why it can matter more than IQ*. New York: Bantam Books.
2. Jensen, A. (1998, April). *Building a role model*. Retrieved December 20, 2000 from EQ Today web site: http://www.eqtoday.com/jpcw98.html.
3. Nelson, P. (1993). *There's a hole in my sidewalk: The romance of self-discovery* (pp. 2–3). Hillsboro, OR: Beyond Words Publishing.

CHAPTER 3: BUILDING RELATIONSHIPS

1. Miller, J. B., & Stiver, I. P. (1997). *The healing connection: How women form relationships in therapy and in life* (p. 26). Boston: Beacon Press.
2. Stern, D. (1985). *The interpersonal world of the infant: A view from psychoanalysis and developmental psychology* (pp. 6–7). New York: Basic Books.
3. Resnick, M. D., & Bearman, P. S. (1997). Protecting adolescents from harm: Findings from the national longitudinal study on adolescent health. *Journal of the American Medical Association, 278*(10), 823–832.
4. Werner, E. E. (1989). High risk children in young adulthood: A longitudinal study from birth to 32 years. *American Journal of Orthopsychiatry, 59*(1), 72–81.
5. Miller, J. B. (1986). *What do we mean by relationships?* (Rep. No. 22)(pp. 1–12). Wellesley, MA: Stone Center, Wellesley College. Jordan, J. V. (1986). *The meaning of mutuality* (Report No. 2)(pp. 1–11). Wellesley, MA: Stone Center, Wellesley College. Surrey, J. (1985). *The "self-in-relation": A theory of women's development* (Rep. No. 13)(pp. 1–10). Wellesley, MA: Stone Center, Wellesley College.

CHAPTER 4: BEING A MEMBER OF A GROUP

1. Goleman, D. (1998). *Working with emotional intelligence* (pp. 199–231). New York: Bantam Books.
2. Knowles, Malcolm & Hulda. (1969). *Understanding group behavior. An introduction to group dynamics* (pp. 1–12). New York: Association Press.

Index

About the Authors

Michelle Seligson has been a nationally recognized leader in child care policy and practice for more than twenty years. She founded the National Institute on Out-of-School Time (NIOST) at Wellesley College's Center for Research on Women and served as its executive director from 1979–1999. Since 1999, Ms. Seligson has served as an associate director of the Center for Research on Women and directs a new project at the Wellesley Centers for Women: Bringing Yourself To Work: Caregiving in After-School Environments, funded by three Boston-area foundations.

Ms. Seligson has been a keynote speaker and featured presenter at many national conferences. She was an invited speaker at the October 1997 White House Conference on Child Care, where she joined President and Mrs. Clinton in stressing the importance of children's out-of-school time. She appeared on the *Today Show* in October 1998, and has also been interviewed on National Public Radio's *All Things Considered*. In addition to numerous articles, her publications include *School-Age Child Care: An Action Manual for the 90s and Beyond* and *Early Childhood Programs and the Public Schools: Between Promise and Practice*. Ms. Seligson holds a B.A. degree in English literature from Simmons College and an Ed.M. in Administration, Planning, and Social Policy from Harvard University Graduate School of Education. She is currently enrolled in the analytic training program at the C. G. Jung Institute of Boston, Massachusetts.

Patricia Jahoda Stahl is an accomplished consultant, trainer, and program developer with over 20 years experience designing and consulting to local and national programs. Prior to her work at the Center for Research on Women at Wellesley College, Pat consulted to the Paul and Phyllis Fireman Charitable Foundation's Girls Action Initiative. For many years, she was the director of adolescent programs at the Boston Children's Museum, during which time she expanded an informal education program that created interactive work opportunities for adolescents in a museum setting. Pat has conducted trainings all over the country in girls' program development, diversity awareness, and prevention initiatives. In 1999, she founded Strategic Philanthropy, a consulting practice in which she assists organizations and foundations in identifying and planning their philanthropic programs.

Pat holds an Ed.M. from Harvard University Graduate School of Education, where she specialized in risk and prevention. Her most recent publications include *Learning from Girls Action: Building Strengths and Saving Self-Esteem in Early Adolescence* and *Growing Together: A Mutual Exchange Between Adolescents and Museums*.